Daniel H Hungr

Everything
a Woman
Needs to Know
to Get Paid
What
She's Worth

EVERYTHING
A WOMAN
NEEDS TO KNOW
TO GET PAID
WHAT
SHE'S WORTH

by Caroline Bird

Edited by

HELENE MANDELBAUM

David McKay Company, Inc.

NEW YORK

Acknowledgments

This book grew out of a course entitled "The Female Job Ghetto" that I conducted at the Center for New York City Affairs of the New School for Social Research in the fall of 1972. Associate Dean Jerome Liblit of the New School got the idea for the course from my article of the same title in *New York* magazine, May 29, 1972. Credit should go, too, to the editors at *MS* magazine who suggested that I compile the examples of unequal pay they published in December 1972.

Helene Mandelbaum's contribution was essentially that of a collaborator. She is identified as the editor on the title page in order to make it clear that the philosophy and resources are mine alone. She made a useful book out of a pile of notes, memos, letters, clips, tapes of conversations and class discussions, and snatches of copy produced by me.

Marge Godfrey was the executive officer of what turned out to be a research enterprise similar to those with which she was familiar at the Rand Corporation. In addition to coordinating the voluminous research and the activities of the many part-time assistants we employed, she pitched in to write, edit, interview, check, and occasionally even to type as needed.

This book was researched, written, and edited simultaneously during an intensive six-month period. It owes more than can be acknowledged to the enthusiasm and resourcefulness of a dozen or more students, housewives, and moonlighting women of diverse skills who pitched in to interview, transcribe tapes, drive copy around, type, look things up in the library, hang on the phone with government officials and other authorities, and generally do what needed doing at the moment. Our "elves," in alphabetical order were: Angela Abbate, Jacquelyn Brown, Liz Cameron, Ollie Carmel, Katherine Du Sault, Karen Hammond, Mary Harrison, Jan Kohler, Marti Madory, Jane Mandelbaum, Doris Morrison, Loretta Petrolino, Eileen Ryan, Lloyd Slater, Liz Stalcup, Esther Vail, and Trudi Willcox.

Four papers submitted by students in my course at the New School were especially helpful. The papers and their authors are: "Black Enterprise" by Ivery Jacobs; "Small Business" by Mary Healey; "Small Business" by Pat McCaffrey; and "Women's Caucuses" by Barbara G. Hirst.

The real authors of this book, of course, are the successful women who provided the answers to the questions that other women ask. Many of them were extremely busy people who took time out early in the morning or late at night to talk with one of us by phone. All were given an opportunity to review that part of their conversation that we have attributed to them, but the quotes are merely the tip of the iceberg. The real guts of the book are the things they told us that we couldn't quote without damaging their careers. Others—both male and female—contributed their knowledge of policy and practices as regulatory officials in the government or personnel specialists in private industry.

Our helpful informants, listed in alphabetical order: Joan Abrams, Margie Albert, Virginia Allen, Ceil Baring-Gould, Karlyn Barker, Lois Baum, Roslyn Beitler, Jane Berry, Joan Bieder, Carol Bird, Sarah Blanding, Mary G. Bodel, Lin Bolen, Clara Bolton, Janet P. Bonnema, Barbara Boyle, Jacqueline Brandwynne, Carolyn Bratt, Joan Breibart, Ruth Brine, Cam Brown, Vera Brown, Dorothy Bryant, M. E. Brydon, Mary Estill Buchanan, Barbara Burns, Virginia Burns, John Butte, Carolyn Buttolph, Aileen Callender, Betty Carroll, Stacy Carter, Bertha Chan, Jane Roberts Chapman, Rona Cherry, Betty Jo Christian, Annie Louise Clay, Blanche Cohen, Roberta Cohen, Laura Collins, Janie Cottrell, Renée Cougle, Loretta Cowden, Bernice Crabtree, Barbara Crosser, Dorothy Ruth Crouch, Agatha Crumb, Jane Currie, Edna Dennis, Diane Devennie, Bobbie Devine, Frances Dias, Suzanne Douglas, Eleanor Driver, Helen Dudley, Joan Durst, Carol Eakle, Catherine East, Jean Faust, Daisy Fields, Kathleen M. Fisher, Jill Flores, Clara Forbes, Charlotte Frank, Philip Freedman, Jim Freeman, Sonia Pressman Fuentes, Helen Galland, Florence Gaynor, Bernice Gera, Sue Geringer, Susan Rogers Giddins, Nellie Gifford, Lela S. Gilbert, Arnold R. Gilbert, Merille Glover, Mary Joan Glynn, Del Goetz, Frances Goldman, Diana Green, Carol Greitzer, Dorothy Haener, Amy Hanan, Betty Harragan, Doris Hardesty, Ruth Harris, Joyce Hartwell, Patricia Haskell, Betty Hawkins, Dourniese Hawkins, Sally Headley, Mary Healey, Susan Hecht, Doris Heflin, Wilma Scott Heide, Marcia de Hellerman, Freda Helphinstine, Mary Lou Hennessy, Susan Hesse, Velma Hill, Donna Hincher, Barbara Hirst, Neal Hoffman, Betsy Hogan, Valerie Howard, Christine Hunter,

Pamela Ilott, Ivery Jacobs, Velma James, Joyce Johnson, William Karp, Jane Kay, Hazel Kellar, Nancy Kelly, Joy Kennedy, Ko Saribekian Kimmel, Pat King, Carol Kleiman, Lucy Komisar, Lester Korn, Mary Kramer, Vicki Kramer, Bette Krenzer, Pat Lane, Gloria Lang, Janice LaRouche, Carol Lehti, Dorothea Lindsay, Anne Lipow, Edith Litt, Diana Loercher, Florence V. Lucas, Clare Boothe Luce, Mary Lum, Lillian Lynch, Naomi McAfee, Jane McCarthy, Ruth McIphenny, Martha McKay, Margaret Maguire, Helene Markoff, Barbara Marshall, Morton Meisler, Pearl Meyer, Bernardine Miller, Joyce Miller, Juliette Moran, Eileen Morley, Elinor Morris, Cathy Morrow, Patricia Neighbors, Christine Nelson, Nancy Nesewich, Elizabeth Osinski, Joan Paylo, Marjorie Paylo, Ann Peabody, Beverly Pearson, Pat Pepin, Nancy Perlman, Hester Phelps, Julianna Prager, Betty Jo Prysi, Mary Ann Quinn, Harriet Rabb, Joel Robinson, Gladys Rogers, Wendy Rue, Lourdes M. Ruiz, Mary Russell, Virginia Sadock, Valerie Salembier, Bernice Sandler, Beth Sapery, Audrey Saphar, Leonard Sayles, Elizabeth Scott, Lucy Sells, Barbara Shack, Lewis Siegel, Morag Simchak, Joanne Simpson, Lella Smith, Helen Smits, Sharon Sopher, Elizabeth Stakelon, Liz Stalcup, Ruth Steinberg, Nancy Sterns, Martha Stuart, Mary Jane Sullivan, Mildred Sussman, Delores Symons, Renée Taft, Nan Talese, Madelon Talley, Mary Tarcher, Carol Tartaglia, Gloria Tate, Amy Terry, Ann Thomas, Yvonne Treadwell, Maggie Tripp, Antonina Uccello, Susan Van Voorhis, Beverley Wadsworth, Lee Walker, Julia Montgomery Walsh, Lois Weed, Ruth Weiner, Bonnie Weiss, Arlene Wenig, Barbara Wertheimer, Ruth Weyand, Donald J. White, Martha White, Rabbi Solomon L. Williger, Darlene Willoughby, Fred Young, Genevieve Young.

Finally, Helene, Marge, and I want to thank our respective husbands, Harold Mandelbaum, Richard Godfrey, and Tom Mahoney, for unfailing and unpaid assistance, ranging from messenger service to moral support and the perspective that can be provided only by the other, but definitely not the second, sex.

Caroline Bird
Poughkeepsie, New York
February 18, 1973

Contents

Everything a Woman Needs to Know to Get Paid What She's Worth

1

The Female Job Ghetto

This book is for women who work, and 33 million of them do. This book is for women who want to be paid what they are worth. Most women work for less.

It is not a book to help women decide whether they should work, or whether they should choose to be full-time housewives and mothers. It is for those women who have made the choice, who are—or will be—working at some kind of paid employment, and who want to earn money commensurate with their abilities.

They are tired of being asked why they want to work. Nobody ever asks a man his reason for working.

They are tired of being told that they can't expect to earn as much as a man because they don't have a family to support. Most of them do. No one ever suggests to a single man, or to a man with a working wife, that he should be satisfied with less money than a man who is the sole support of a large family.

They don't need any more advice on how to care for their children or households when they do work. Nobody ever asks a man about his housekeeping arrangements.

This is not a book about how to succeed on the job. There is a world of literature about getting into and up out of good jobs, and anyone who hasn't delved into this "success" literature should take a look at what the students of getting ahead say about how to write a résumé, how to put your best foot forward in a job interview, how to come out with flying colors in a performance review, how and when to ask for a raise, how to win the cooperation of fellow employees, and how, generally, any human being of any sex ought to behave on the job. There is a resource section at the back of the book that lists some of that literature.

This is a book of tactics for dealing with the subtle, omnipresent and unique obstacles women face in demonstrating their competence and in dealing with the male-oriented job world.

How do you know these tactics will work?

These tactics have been reported to us by working women who have used them successfully, and by employment specialists who hire and advise women. We have talked with personnel managers, executive recruiters, vocational counselors, government specialists, and legal experts.

We have talked with several hundred women who hold many different kinds of jobs all over the country. Some of them are now earning good money because they have been able to move out of dead-end jobs; others have set up their own businesses. We talked with women doctors and women plumbers, women who work in offices, and women who work in factories.

Some think that they were discriminated against during their work lives; others feel that they were not. We spoke to women who sued their employers, women who joined unions, and women who said they did nothing but perform very capably on the job. We spoke to women who are achieving now during their twenties, and others who made their breakthrough twenty years ago, and still others who didn't get started until their children were grown. When we wrote down everything they told us, patterns began to emerge. No matter what their education, no matter what their job, no matter how much—or how little—they have earned, women who work do different things from what men do in order to get ahead. What they do, and have done, is the substance of this book.

Why does a woman need special tactics to get paid what she's worth?

There are still some men, and women too, who have outdated notions. Not too long ago, a bright young woman, trained as a systems analyst, was sent by her company to consult at a customer's data-processing department. The client/manager met her at the door and said, "You might as well turn right around and go on back to your office. Your fee is $20 an hour, and no woman is worth that much—standing up."

Isn't it enough for a woman to be very good at what she does?

Successful women really believe so, but they don't realize how much of their success comes from the way they manage their competence. Almost everybody knows some dedicated woman who works twice as hard and is

twice as good as anybody else in sight and who winds up
with nothing but grief for her efforts. A woman who
wants to get paid what she's worth can learn a lot by
analyzing what the dedicated martyrs do wrong.

Mary Jones—that's not her name—has a responsible
job in one of the big Federal regulatory agencies. Everyone admits she is not only competent, but sometimes
brilliant at interpreting and enforcing the complex regulations she administers. Her work takes her all over the
country, and although she exercises considerable power
over businessmen, they universally respect her fairness
as well as her competence.

Many of them add that they find her easier to deal with
than the younger men who do the same job. Mary gets
A for diligence and excellence from her colleagues in
Washington, too. She always volunteers for the knottiest
problems, takes them home to study, and comes up with
creative solutions. She is a perfectionist. Rather than
tolerate the sloppiness of the secretarial services available in her agency, she types the reports herself. During
the twenty years she has spent in the Federal service she
has taken all the advanced training and professional degrees available under Civil Service educational leave and
reimbursement plans, so she has a far more impressive
professional background than the young men on her
level. She is the senior professional in her category, and
ought to be the head of the department. Instead, she has
suffered every form of discrimination of which feminists
complain. She has been passed over for promotion. She
has been denied information, so that it is harder for her
to do her job well. She is sometimes at the bottom of a
routed memo so that she doesn't get important agency
news in time. Women clerical workers sabotage her.
They put work she gives them on the bottom of the pile,

and she is afraid that they listen in on her phone calls in hopes of picking up gossip they can use against her.

How does she cope? With the men who exclude her, she never makes an issue of it. "I try to do things indirectly." With the women secretaries who do sloppy work because they resent her, she "sticks with standards even though they like the men better because they let the girls get away with a lot more." She won't compromise, even when it means doing her own typing.

This approach has obviously been counterproductive. By taking it both from men and from women, she has become bitter, resentful, and defensive, thus stimulating more of the same ostracism that she complains about.

She has a good relationship with the clients of her agency—the businessmen it regulates—which suggests that getting along with other people is not her problem.

What is wrong? Her own diagnosis is that she does her job so well that she shows the others up and that is why they resent her. She does not recognize that she is a victim of put-downs primarily because she does not take positive steps to assert her professional role. The majority of women we interviewed would have told her to spend some of her energy making an issue of her status with her male colleagues and enforcing agency discipline on the secretaries instead of doing their work for them. She prefers the role of martyr, and it is self-defeating.

I don't want to be president of the company. All I want is to make a decent living. Why do I need to know how to get ahead?

We wouldn't talk any woman into changing her life for the world. The choice of how high a woman aims, what she wants to do with her life, and what kind of work she wants to do, is hers alone. All we care about is that every woman gets fairly rewarded for what she does choose to do.

But we must add that it is not quite as simple as that. It is very hard for a woman to know how high she really would like to go if she had the opportunity. Take, for instance, this business of money.

"I'm more interested in a job I like than in making money," a professional woman once told me. But when a duller and less prestigious firm offered her more money, she switched without demur. No woman knows for sure whether she would rather have a higher-paying job until she gets the chance to turn one down. Most women don't get that chance so they never find out. But one thing is certain: nothing raises sights so fast as the assurance that it is possible for you to be paid what you are worth.

Why are most women underpaid?

Employers pay many women less than they are worth to the enterprise simply because they can get them for less. The daily paper may be worth a dollar to many people, but they buy it for fifteen cents like everyone else.

So with women. Women work cheaper than men because they are arbitrarily limited to "women's jobs," where they compete with each other, thereby driving their wages down. Men have a wider choice of jobs. When a man is not satisfied with the salary he is getting, he can quit to take a better-paying job.

Women have fewer options than men. They have to work for less because they are occupationally restricted. They are forced to work in a female job ghetto.

Why do people call it a job ghetto?

Because the job market has very visible walls. Male occupations are a turf from which women are excluded. Female occupations are a reservation from which women stray at their own risk. A typing pool, a teachers' meeting, a telephone switchboard, a nursing station, or the employee cafeteria of a big store sounds, feels, and even smells like a women's rest room, a convent, or for all we know, a Middle-Eastern harem. The atmosphere differs from that of the locker room of a football team, the board room of a big corporation, the day room of a police station, or a construction job compound for men only. Men build their own barriers; women have no choice—they are confined to women's jobs because they have not been allowed anywhere else.

What is a woman's job?

There is a simple way to define it. Whatever the duties are—and they vary from place to place and from time to time—a woman's job is anything that pays less than a man will do it for.

Aren't there laws that prevent women from being underpaid?

Yes. Discrimination against women on the job is not only unfair, it is also illegal.

1. The Equal Pay Act of 1963, amended in 1972, requires almost every employer to pay equal salaries and wages for equal work without regard to sex.

2. Title VII, of the Civil Rights Act of 1964, amended in 1972 by the Equal Employment Opportunity Act, prohibits any employer, employment agency, or union from discriminating in any way on the basis of sex.

3. Executive Order 11246 of 1965, amended by 11375 in 1967, prohibits discrimination by most employers who have contracts with the Federal government.

Revised Order 4, issued in 1971, mandates that women must be included in affirmative action plans, which are required of all Federal contractors. These plans must establish, in writing, specific goals, procedures, and timetables for correcting the underrepresentation of women and minority workers in every job category.

Any woman who feels she is being underpaid, and/or discriminated against on the job, may take her case to the government, and to court if necessary. We will tell her exactly how to do this in chapter 11 of this book.

However, it takes a very long time, before laws, no matter how well enforced, can change ingrained custom, and there are many other things an individual woman can do to make more money without taking the legal route. And while she is doing them, it is a comfort to know that the law is on her side.

With all those laws, how can women get paid less than men?
Women lose out in very specific ways:
- *Same title, lower pay.* Some companies still have different pay scales for men and women doing the same job. Blatant differentials are now illegal, of course, but many employers—and the women who work for them—have not yet caught up with the law. However, even when the starting salaries are the same, women are less apt to get merit increases. Thus they usually average lower pay than men with the same title, particularly in bureaucratic organizations that provide for increases within grade.
- *Same work, different title carrying lower pay.* It's easy to

call a man in a personnel department who sees job applicants an "interviewer," and pay him more than a woman who does the same but is called a "clerk." If a man is the administrative assistant to the president of a company he is usually paid more than the president's secretary, even though she is equally adept at solving problems for her employer, and probably knows more about the company because she has been there longer. Male "janitors" always have been paid more than female "maids."

This evasion of the Equal Pay Act has been tested and found illegal, and an employer cannot muddy the waters by asking the janitor to do a little extra heavy work. Since 1970 the courts have held that the "skill, effort and responsibility" of the jobs compared must be "substantially equal" rather than identical. This means that an employer can no longer send a male bank teller to an occasional field investigation, call him a trainee, and pay him more than a female bank teller. But it will be a long time before all these irregularities are uncovered, and meanwhile, the women continue to earn less money.

• *Same work, same pay, different qualifications.* Women frequently discover that they are better educated and more qualified than men doing the same work. Econometric studies of wage differentials show that women workers usually have more education and experience than the men on their level.

• *Same qualifications, lower pay.* Women get assigned to the lower-paying jobs in a field because more women than men are available. An article in a chemical-industry trade publication reports that women are found in the lowest-paying jobs requiring the degree—pharmaceuticals, research, and high-school teaching. Male chemists tend to be in management or administration, production, inspection, and the industrial jobs that pay better.

The article adds that the pay gap between male and female chemists widened between 1968 and 1970.

Another good example is the market for academic women in big metropolitan centers such as New York City and Berkeley, where many women Ph.D.'s are married to men Ph.D.'s or men employed in the professions in these cities. Since the women can't move as easily as the men, they are available for the lower-paid academic jobs. One female professor at a metropolitan college thinks that, unconsciously at least, heads of departments in big city universities encourage a large crop of women Ph.D.'s because they know that they will be available to do the assisting and research scutwork—the intellectual slave labor on which so much academic work is based.

• *Same work, different opportunities for promotion.* Women get lower pay than men because they are passed over for promotion to jobs carrying higher pay. The new laws prohibit this also, but it will be a long time before even enlightened organizations compensate for the discrepancies of the past.

• *Same job, different organization.* Women are more apt to work in small, new, and marginal enterprises than in the big, old, rich ones that pay better. Worse yet, women drag each other down. Office workers get less in companies that employ women alone in this category than they get in companies which employ both sexes.

In an exhaustive investigation of the differences in hourly earnings between men and women, Victor R. Fuchs, vice-president of the National Bureau of Economic Research, found that the higher the percentage of female employment in an occupation or industry, the lower the earnings. This was true for the men in predominantly female industries as well as for the women.

• *Different jobs, lower pay.* Most women work in women's jobs. In 1969 one fourth of all employed women were in five occupations—secretary-stenographer, household worker, bookkeeper, elementary-school teacher, and waitress. Secretaries' and stenographers' jobs alone accounted for one in every ten women workers.

Dr. Fuchs was struck by how very few occupations employ large numbers of both sexes. "Most men are employed in occupations that employ very few women, and a significant fraction of women work in occupations that employ very few men."

More simply, where the men are, that's where the money is.

How are women kept in ghetto jobs?

Women intuitively know and observe the invisible bars that keep them in typing, teaching, clerking, and nursing. But for those who would stray off the reservation, there are a number of sanctions. First is the assumption that no woman could possibly ask for such a job. When the first woman was admitted to membership in the New York Stock Exchange, the governors discovered, to their embarrassment, that no special action was required, because women had not been specifically barred. The authors of the constitution of that venerable body did not think it necessary to specify the sex of "members." Obviously, of course, they would be male.

The remedy, of course, is to challenge the assumptions, and this is the service that has been performed by the militants and the pioneers. Bernice Gera, the pioneer baseball umpire, admits that she fought for the right to be an umpire, rather than the job itself. She got herself accepted at umpire school because the head of the school thought the letter of application had come from a man. When she had to call him on the phone, and he realized that his applicant was Bernice, not "Bernie," he bellowed that there had never been a woman in his umpire school and there never would be.

Another way of maintaining the job ghetto is to juggle the specifications of nonghetto jobs so that women are excluded, just as real-estate covenants force blacks into the central city even when they can afford to live in suburbs.

Physical specifications are a case in point. Bernice Gera eventually was turned down because at 5 feet, 2 inches, she was "too small." She took her case to court and won her contention that height was not relevant to her duties. Two visual-aid specialists, employed by New York City's Hunter College and Hunter High School respectively, were not so fortunate. They were threatened with demotion from jobs they had been successfully doing when they were unable to raise a 25-pound bar bell overhead in one hand in the course of a surprise physical examination. The same test required them, among other things, to run an obstacle course in 20 seconds, starting from prone position. The city department which administers the Civil Service exam says that they have to be able to lift heavy equipment in and out of cars. The women have challenged the qualifications in court.

2

Women in Men's Jobs

How can a woman earn more money?

She has to go where the men are—in the professions, in management, in white-collar jobs. If it's a man's job, the women who do it earn more than they would in a woman's job. If the industry or occupation employs more men than women, the women who do manage to get in earn more than in an industry where women predominate. In the clothing and related industries, where 70 percent of the workers are women, 1969 wages averaged $78 weekly. In chemicals and certain leather products, where women are only 22 percent and 11 percent of the workers respectively, weekly wages were $139 and $133.

Publishing is the field in New York City that has the highest proportion of women managers and professionals. The salaries they earn are lower than those of

managers and professionals in a similar field, like advertising, where there are fewer women at the top.

*How does a woman get into a male-dominated organization or
profession or trade?*
        She finds a "woman's angle" or "feminizes" the job.
Women who work at "men's jobs" have always found
reasons—valid or not—to explain why they would be
good at some particular job, whether they are doctors or
plumbers.

Policewomen point out that in a tense situation, the
presence of a woman frequently defuses violence.
Women journalists exaggerate the "woman's angle" in
politics in order to get to interview Presidential candidates.

In the past, women lawyers have been funneled into
trusts and estates on the theory that a woman understands the needs of widows and minors better than a man
does. But now that women are demanding entry into
such masculine strongholds as criminal law—with its
connotations of toughness and violence—Mary B.
Tarcher, assistant attorney-in-chief at the New York Legal Aid Society, points out that "women lawyers have
often been known to keep their cool better than do some
of the male attorneys. The expertise of women shows up
in their objectivity."

The president of a California junior college claims she
was able to settle a nasty labor dispute that flared up on
her campus because the foul-mouthed, but sexist union
leader was so put off when he discovered he was going
to have to deal with a woman that he couldn't think of
a thing to say without his usual expletives.

A woman hearing examiner in a Federal regulatory

agency thinks she is better respected than the men doing her job (she is the only woman) because "a woman is more sensitive to other people's feelings. I try never to embarrass attorneys."

Women are beginning to break into horse racing with the argument that they have always liked horses better than men do, and tender loving care counts in grooming. Donna Hincher, a pioneer woman groom, says that a famous thoroughbred trainer prefers girl grooms because they are conscientious and neater, and she adds Freudian reasons, too. As the weaker sex, females are supposed to enjoy the mastery of dominating a big and fast animal. Men sometimes add that the rhythm of galloping is like sexual intercourse.

Small numbers of women have always gone into medicine, but they are just beginning to enter dentistry in any numbers, and one woman in a dental college says women make good dentists because they have a tender touch— and because they are good at matching colors for dentures and crowns!

Bertha Chan, who owns and operates Century Plumbers in Los Angeles, makes the most of her ability to advise on styles when installing bathroom or kitchen fixtures.

The ultimate in "feminizing" is probably the contention of a pioneer bail bondswoman that the occupation needed a woman because people accused of crime deserve special sympathy.

Isn't it contradictory to "feminize" a job when you don't really believe that women are all that different?

Possibly, but it is the first step in breaking down sex roles. When change is necessary, practical reformers know better than to attack ingrained beliefs directly. They work with them. That's the way missionaries introduced Christianity to primitives, and in our own country the way county agents got old-fashioned farmers to adopt new methods. Practically speaking, people may need reasons for anything—particularly for a change in custom—so finding reasons why a woman is better may be a better strategy than the truth, which is that sex does not make the difference. A woman who is going to be a social pioneer should do what the successful feminists in the past have done: start where the male chauvinists are, and broaden their experience.

Is it always possible to "feminize" a job?

Almost always. In spite of the splendid institution of the British barmaid, bartending has been regarded as so inappropriate for women in the United States that many states prohibit them from doing it. This has deprived women of a job that pays more, and brings higher tips than similar jobs in which women serve food as well as drinks at tables. One of the reasons for the "men only" rule behind the bar has been that it allegedly takes a man to eject drunks. Another reason, of course, is that traditionally the bar is a refuge from women.

Now that women are demanding bartending jobs, they have found a good reason why they are better at this work than men: the pioneer women bartenders say they have an easier time jollying drunks out of the place than men do. In order to demonstrate, Phyllis Seidman, twenty-four, went to work on a television newsman who was simulating an unruly customer, took him by the arm and propelled him out of the door of the White Horse Inn in New York City, to which she was applying for a job as bouncer. "Most men are a lot less liable to try to prove their masculinity by belting a woman," said Ellen Sigward, another applicant.

There's a lot of heavy industry in our area, and the men who work in it earn good money. Can a woman "feminize" a job like that?

Yes, if she likes to work with her hands. Janie Cottrell is a welder who works for Scientific-Atlanta, Inc., in Georgia. She was urged to take a welding course in vocational school by a teacher who knew how unhappy she was in a business program. He assured her that women could be better welders than men because their hands are steadier.

She caught on to welding very quickly, and found that she liked it. "To me, welding is an art and a science," she says. The necessary skills are those that are usually called "feminine"—finger and hand dexterity, eye-hand coordination (abilities that are necessary for typing), plus an aptitude for form and space perception.

Tests of high-school students have actually shown that the combination of aptitudes required for a number of crafts and trades, including office-machine repair, radio and television repair, automobile mechanics, aircraft mechanics, and household-appliance repair are found as frequently among female students as among their male counterparts. And many of these trades do not require physical strength beyond the capacities of large numbers of women.

Janie Cottrell now makes more money than she would have if she had continued with the business course, and she is in a line of work that she enjoys. "I would never have stayed working inside an office," she says.

Isn't it hard to be the first woman in a trade?

It's hard to be the first woman anywhere. Before Janie Cottrell was hired as a welder, the foreman made her demonstrate her ability. He was skeptical until she welded a strip, and then he announced that she did it better than a lot of men.

Dourniese Hawkins, a Con Edison gas mechanic, was not interested in pioneering—she just liked outdoor work. She thinks, as do many women pioneers, that she has to be better at her job, so she tries harder.

She also believes in speaking up. If the boss is wrong, she tells him. She once argued with her boss about the length of pipe that should be used for a connection, and won her point when she used her knowledge of mechanical technology, which she had studied at Staten Island Community College.

She also tries to be a good sport. Some men accept her, others do not. She recalls one man who was furious that she and he were on the same work crew. He ordered her around as if he were an Army sergeant, but it did not bother her at all. "He's just one of those men who has trouble relating to anyone on the job, male or female."

Sometimes the problem is a semantic one. Marilyn Rothfuss, Con Edison's pioneer woman meter reader, says she's darned if she'll call out, "gas girl," just because the men say,"gas man" when they knock on a door. She introduces herself as "Con Edison."

How do women break into a field where there never have been any women before?

Sometimes just because they are a novelty, but then everyone discovers they are an asset. One of the spin-offs of the Women's Liberation Movement has been to create these pioneering opportunities, either because of equal opportunity laws, or because the thought of opening jobs to women has occurred either to an employer or a woman. Out in Coronado, California, a Navy town, Jon Duringer thought that women car salesmen might jazz up his automobile agency, so he put an ad in the local paper advising women that "If you're willing to work, I'm willing to teach." Sixty women applied.

The women have been a great success. "We get better women for the money," Duringer says. "They take the training more seriously and go through the prescribed sales procedures more systematically. After all, there are very few jobs that a woman can get without extensive training that pay from $800 to $1200 a month."

Florence Gaynor of Newark, New Jersey, the first woman to head a major nonsectarian hospital, thinks that luck has a lot to do with it. "You have to be in the right place at the right time," she says.

The classic explanation of "first woman" is some emergency or extremity for which using women appears to be a solution. Then, when the women do the job as well as men, to the surprise of everyone, they are kept on.

I'd like to get into police work. How do you "feminize" that?

This is one category in which "feminizing" has been very successful. Women are now in protection and police work all over the country.

They do patrol work and detective work on police forces. They are in the F.B.I., they are investigating mail frauds, protecting the President and his family, and tracking down drug pushers. Talk to the first women and their bosses and you wonder why it has taken so long to discover that women were needed: virtually every one of them is doing work that makes her sex an asset.

Criminals don't expect a woman to be on their trail, so a woman is better at surveillance than a man. A woman calms down a little toddler in a house where she and her partner are making an arrest. Sometimes she can get information out of a suspect or a witness more easily. Or pose as a call girl to keep a dangerous criminal occupied in a male "key" club. One young woman doing under-cover work says that police work fulfills her longtime ambition to be an actress and she also notes that mixed teams—a man and a woman—are less conspicuous.

Did the men who run protection agencies and police forces suddenly realize that women would be effective? Hardly. They changed their minds about women firing guns because of the new equal opportunity laws.

The Federal Bureau of Investigation was forced by a law suit to accept women agents. But the moral is clear: Whenever sex is used as a qualification—either to keep women out of a job or to keep them penned into one— rationalizations spring up to validate the policy.

Not all women want to be mechanics, engineers, or policewomen. What can a woman do to get out of the job ghetto in the business world?

Again, she has to go where the men are, and find an aspect of her industry or organization in which males predominate. Joan Breibart, an executive with a publish-ing company, broke out of the editorial work to which so many women are confined by undertaking to sell print-ing and binding on commission, a job usually reserved for men.

An important career advantage of a "man's job" is that

it provides visibility. Most women's jobs are designed to be invisible: back room, assistant to, research. Women do the essential work whose contribution can't be measured easily. It's hard to prove just what a "girl Friday" contributes. Everyone knows what a salesman does. He or she can tot it up on an adding machine and present a bill.

This is easiest to see in fields where the business depends on selling clients, such as stock brokerage, management consulting, accounting. The big pay goes to the salesmen, while the duties that are not visible, such as managing the paperwork in a brokerage firm, are left to women. That's their ghetto.

In other fields, the promotion department is the ghetto. The work has to be done, but you can't measure contribution, and very few company presidents rise from the public relations department.

By no accident, public relations employs a higher percentage of women than finance, marketing, division management, or administration. And these, according to Eugene Jennings, a student of management, are the "top four rungs of the corporate ladder, from which executives are being promoted today."

Aspiring men are advised by employment counselors to get into these areas—and the advice makes equally good sense for aspiring women.

The newspapers are full of feature stories on women who have big jobs these days—aren't they finally breaking into top management?

Don't hold your breath. There is a slight improvement in the percentage of women in the highest salary brackets in the 1970 census, but when you allow for inflation, and a general shift toward the higher brackets, the improvement is hard to see with the naked eye.

Statistically speaking, the male domination of the top continues undented. There was not a single woman on the rosters of the highest-paid executives of 1971 compiled by *Forbes* and *Business Week* from proxy statements.

How do you "feminize" a top corporate job?

By preaching and practicing the new style of management that the business schools and management consultants are promoting. It grows out of the task-force approach that was developed for the space program, and is now being used in many industries.

The task force is the new look in hospitals, where teams of cooperating health-care specialists of random sex are replacing the authoritarian male doctor and his subservient female nurse. And while hospitals are becoming less authoritarian, they are also becoming less male dominated: in the early 1970s, women were still rare in top hospital jobs, but many were training for hospital management.

One of the first management consultants to see the advantage women enjoy in this new climate is Mary Estill Buchanan, management consultant, graduate of the Harvard Business School, and mother of six children. She points out that today's successful executive "is more of an egalitarian leader than a Prussian officer."

Not only is this a more comfortable role for a woman, but Ms. Buchanan suggests that successful women are particularly adept at living with the stresses of top management, where "a high tolerance for ambiguity, and a high threshold for coping with uncertain circumstances" is essential. Women can do this because they have developed tactics for coping with such situations in their juggling of home-work conflicts.

Juliette Moran, senior vice-president of the GAF Corporation, practices this style. "I try not to give orders," she says. "I always try to define problems."

According to Leonard Sayles, professor of management at the Columbia Graduate School of Business, "much of the real decision-making in organizations takes place behind the scenes, where you negotiate, or persuade, or influence, and women have lots of early training and cultural indoctrination in being sensitive to the hidden cues that represent the real resistance of the persons whom they are persuading."

How can a woman break into top management?

By paying attention to money matters. Juliette Moran credits much of her rise in the chemically based GAF Corporation to the knowledge of accounting she acquired on her initial job in research and development. Her grasp of costs and profits made her valuable as she moved up in management.

Barbara Marshall, president of Welcome Wagon International, headquartered in Memphis, Tennessee, says she was regarded as something of a freak on her way up in a number of major corporations because she was good at making money. She left Revlon, in spite of the freedom its middle-management women had, because they were denied financial information. "When I was dealing with the sales department, they wouldn't tell me what they were willing to spend to put the product across," she recalls. "I couldn't make a sensible recommendation about marketing without knowing about the money."

Tactic: Learn all you can about the financial affairs of your organization.

Is there an advantage to being a woman in a top job?

Joanne Simpson, who runs a U.S. weather-research laboratory in Florida, has made the most of her uniqueness. Says she, "Since I'm the only woman at my level, I can be the licensed lunatic Bertrand Russell talks about."

A woman may find herself excluded from regular channels, but she can also escape their frustrations. Several women have claimed that they are more forthright than the etiquette of work allows men in their jobs to be.

Women frequently go over the heads of their bosses and get away with it. There is a wonderful story about the former president of Vassar, Sarah Blanding. When she was dean of the College of Home Economics at Cornell, she forgot to tell the president that she had asked for outside money with which to carry on some war research. When summoned to account for this breach of etiquette, she crawled into the president's office on all fours, carrying a check for $100,000 from the state of New York. The president dissolved in laughter. A man could never have gotten away with that.

I've been offered a job in a new company—and I think they're hiring me because they think that a woman will get them publicity. Should I take it?

Absolutely. "There's nothing wrong with being a gimmick woman," says Suzanne Douglas, who made her reputation as a female space-sales representative on a new magazine. The publisher thought it would be cute to hire a woman to sell advertising space for a woman's magazine—something previously unheard of. Because the magazine was a new one with a minuscule sales force, she had her choice of accounts, including the big ones that women were never allowed to solicit. The small number of women who sold advertising space on other publications or in other media, ordinarily were assigned to travel, mail-order, or other potentially small accounts with small commissions. (Every field, even the most masculine, which excludes virtually all women, has its own little ghetto for the ladies.)

Aren't some women given fancy titles, just so the company can say that they don't discriminate?

Yes. Those women are tokens. Although the blacks, women, and young people who are appearing on boards of directors of big companies may beef about their role, they all agree that the visibility gained for their group is worth the indignity of being taken as a symbol.

The personal hazards are hostility from fellow blacks, women, or youths, who suspect that the token has sold out to the interests, or who are frankly envious of the token's income and prestige. This tempts the token to represent his or her group so militantly that he or she cannot take full advantage of the opportunities the high position offers.

Token appointments have launched some brilliant women. Patricia Harris, the black lawyer who presided over the credentials committee of the 1972 Democratic National Convention, got her start as Ambassador to Luxembourg which had become a token-for-women post. Subsequently, she was appointed to the board of IBM, where she represented both blacks and women.

One career hazard of being a token is the tendency of colleagues or superiors or potential employers to regard a token as "nothing but a token." This is implicit in the defensive comment, "But she's a good lawyer, really" or "she does a good job"—as if she were not really expected to be competent or do a good job.

Another drawback is that a token may be promoted too fast to get the experience needed for real competence. It is no service to a black or a woman to be jumped several steps into a job that he or she is unable—and hence not expected—to do.

Do you have to be a militant feminist to be a token?

Not at all. Tokens frequently break with the Women's Liberation Movement. Jean Westwood, the former Democratic National Chairman, was "proud to be your chairman." She didn't call herself a chairperson or a chairwoman. Yet she helped to break forever the stereotype that you can't have a woman in the chair. Millions who watched on television saw her and other women preside gracefully over one of the most unruly big gatherings in American history.

A token has to look "feminine," or there's no point. When Jayne Baker Spain, the vice-chairman of the U.S Civil Service Commission, was running her own company, she had white French provincial furniture in her office.

A good token woman ought to be reassuring to moderates and even to sexist men, but she no longer needs to be frilly. A friend is quoted as saying of Ms. Westwood that "she is the type of person who can let her hair go for ten days if it means working at headquarters, yet she can look great in the black llama coat Christian Dior designed for her."

The women chosen as tokens are socially and politically conservative.

"No company wants a woman who gets up on a soapbox," says Martha Clampitt McKay, a corporate community relations specialist who has assisted American Telephone and Telegraph and other corporations in identifying qualified women for board positions. Women on the boards can be evidence not only of equal opportunity and a concern for providing role models for women employees at the very top, but as evidence of a concern for consumer, community, and minority demands on business.

Being the first woman on the job may get someone a lot of publicity, but will all those men accept her?

Almost all pioneer women say that they have more trouble from their associates than they do from customers, clients, or outsiders. The pioneer car saleswomen found that any resistance on the part of the customers was much less of a problem than the resistance of fellow salesmen. This is true for other pioneers as well: customers are not as much of a problem to women stockbrokers as are other brokers in the office. Women lawyers have more problems with other lawyers than with clients. And Bernice Gera, the pioneer baseball umpire, was tormented, not by the ballplayers, but by other umpires.

Madelon Talley, the first portfolio manager for one of the Dreyfus funds, says that she got much more help from acquaintances in the financial community whom she had met when she was assistant to the boss, than she did from other fund managers. There is a certain amount of competition among people doing the same work, and very often women do not fit into the rather masculine, clubby ways in which men on the same level deal with their competition.

This can lead to loneliness. It was one of the trials Bernice Gera had to bear at umpire school. Women students in architecture, engineering, and even business-administration schools make the same complaint. If there are very few women, or only one, fellow students may not even want to date her. Deprived of female companionship, the woman may even lose out on male companionship. It's the same on the job. The one woman professional is left out of lunching.

And take the common ploy of ignoring what women say. It's done to policewomen by their bosses; it's done to lawyers by judges. Or they are left to fend for themselves on the job. The first women to drive patrol cars were put on patrol without being given any instructions. The first women to attend medical school were required to lecture on male sexual anatomy with a view to embarrassing them. When I went to work as a copy-desk editor for the New York *Journal of Commerce*, nobody told me how to do the job. A linotype man—not someone on the editorial side—told me how to make up the page.

I'm the first woman in my position in our company, but everybody seems to want to protect me from doing my job. I'm afraid they'll "protect" me right out of it. Will it ever end?

After a woman gets a man's job, sometimes she has to keep pioneering to be allowed to do it. According to Catherine Milton's landmark report "Women in Policing," policemen have been so fearful of harm coming to policewomen serving as decoys that they have let the criminal go. If they can get along without the "burden" of a woman to be protected, they would rather. The result is that policewomen have been relegated whenever possible to secretarial and inside duties, where they become sitting ducks for the complaint that they are not earning their pay. This happens despite orders against using policewomen as secretaries.

In 1972 women postal guards won the right to equal duties with the men. "Now we are finding out that it isn't so nice to stand out in the rain or cold," says Darlene Willoughby, one of the first women to be hired in the security force of the San Francisco postal service. "But if I am needed out in the field somewhere, that is where I want to be."

One of our pioneers suggests that a woman who thinks she's being handled with kid gloves should try to be blunt about it. She should tell the men with whom she works that she really wants to know how she's doing her job. She can point out that their bending over backwards to protect her is actually a handicap.

Is it always a hassle to be the "first woman"?

No. The majority of the pioneers have the same experience. They encounter disbelief, embarrassment, and sometimes hazing. But once they prove their worth —and it may take only a day or so—they are regarded as somehow better than they are. The reasoning is "She can do it, so she must be a very unusual woman."

I've had loan officers of banks, stockbrokers, television producers, and civil engineers tell me of their first days at work and it's always the same. There will be a few hours—or at the most a few days—of strain, but then it's clear sailing. One pioneer said, "It's rough to be the first woman, but it's also terrific, because everybody sees you."

"I was a little reluctant about riding with a female partner," admitted patrolman C. E. Daniel, a black policeman, "but after a few hours I relaxed and realized that it had a great psychological effect on people in general."

Sometimes the men on a job will haze a woman, much as they would any other newcomer. A woman engineer who had to climb up the "Christmas tree" of a petroleum refinery tells how the men made it hard for her at first, then accepted her when she "passed" their test. It was like initiation into a fraternity.

And sometimes the shock value of a woman's presence is an asset in itself. Madelon Talley, manager of one of the Dreyfus investment funds, says, "There are so few women doing my work that I tend to stand out." The fund she manages has European investors who are apt to be more prejudiced than Americans against women. She says that they are so surprised that she is a woman that they remember her.

Twenty-five-year-old Judy Hird, the first woman to serve as a pastor in a Lutheran church in the United States, says that people are "very interested in the fact that I am a woman, and for that reason, they are more apt to listen to me than to someone to whom they're accustomed." It's one way to get people out to church!

Isn't it hard to follow a "first woman"? She's usually so good that you'd have to be a superwoman to match her.

Not necessarily. It's actually easier to be second—or third—than first, and it's also easier to become the "first woman" in your company if someone else has already pioneered in a similar company.

Way back when I wrote *Born Female,* I discovered that

employers are like sheep. In some cities, all the banks had women vice-presidents. In others, there wasn't a one. Inevitably, when one bank installed a woman and started crowing about it, the bank across the street felt obliged to match it.

It's fine to say that you're better off going into a man's job, but what do you do about public opinion?

More young women all the time are turning the joke back on the jokesters. Ann Landers had a snappy reply for an eighteen-year-old girl who wrote she was being kidded by friends when she told them she intended to go to college and become a mortician: "Hang in there. You could be the one to give them their last put-down."

Can a woman really be "good at" a traditionally male job?

Of course. Many women hate offices and have no bent for teaching, although too many discover this only when they try one of the proper "women's jobs." Almost as many women as men have a natural aptitude for mathematics and mechanics, many psychologists believe, before the aptitude is trained out of them. If the so-called sex-role "brainwashing" does not take on a girl with such aptitudes, she will be drawn to engineering, construction, or one of the mechanical trades.

Janet P. Bonnema, now an engineering technician with the state highway department of Colorado, went to work for Boeing in Seattle when she discovered that she didn't like teaching and couldn't earn a decent living any other way with a bachelor's degree in history from the University of Colorado. Her first job at Boeing was in the respectably feminine personnel department at $73 a week, but as she processed applications for engineers and discovered that they were all making more money than she was, she transferred into engineering. She went back to college for physics and math courses that qualified her to become an engineering technician.

Aren't women who go into masculine jobs considered "unladylike" and aggressive?

Not at all. It just means that women who are naturally aggressive, women who like outdoor work, women who like athletics, are able to express these preferences and find work congenial to them.

A long-term trend, visible in daily life, has been the growing participation of women in active sports—in hot, sweaty-type sports formerly regarded as "unladylike." It's part of the tendency toward less sex segregation in recreation, with more women going camping and fishing with their husbands. Roberta Cohen, recently appointed assistant director of athletics at the City College of New York, thinks that "the interest in active sports was always there" during the ten years she has worked in athletics, "but now women are saying more about it." She was appointed to her job, a post previously held by men, because the college administration felt that women should be represented in athletics.

If I join the Navy will people think I'm a butch?

A woman always runs that risk when she takes on a man's job, but there are ways of coping with the put-down.

People vulgar enough to circulate rumors about another person's sexual orientation are also ignorant enough to think that you can recognize it by the way a woman dresses. One of the women craftsmen in a blue-collar trade makes a point of wearing long skirts and frilly blouses when she is not working in her shop. Mary Ann Quinn, a steeplejack, wears high heels when she's not climbing, a practice that once made a school superintendent whose flagpole she was going to paint wonder whether she really could climb up it. Both make a point of referring to their husbands when the subject of family life comes up.

Carol Lehti, associate director of ABC sports, says she gets the question of sexual orientation thrown at her all the time. People can't imagine a woman doing her job who isn't a lesbian. "If I see that they are prying to find out which sex I like, I just tell them that my private life is my own business."

Can a woman get out of the ghetto without pioneering in a man's job?

Yes. She can do "women's work" in a man's world. Every woman who gains a foothold in a man's field helps to rectify the lopsided sex and pay ratio even if, as is most likely, she gets in by doing a "feminine" job. The company nurse and recreation directors and the powerful female executive secretary to the president help to break down the "stag" atmosphere of a steel rolling mill, even though they are admitted to these male preserves because they are doing jobs it is imagined only women can do.

A good recent example of pioneering is Marilyn L. Pierce, a twenty-year-old medic who is the first to serve with an Air Force air-rescue team. She is lowered from the rescue helicopter on a hoist cable to administer first aid to people who are injured in locations where the helicopter cannot land.

Many new opportunities for women exist now in the job areas and industries that have developed out of work women used to do in their homes, such as caring for the sick (health), bringing up children (education), or caring for the disadvantaged (welfare).

If you look for the health, education, and welfare angle, aren't you reinforcing stereotypes that say women should stay in women's work?

No, you are being practical. The women doctors who tend to be clustered in pediatrics, women lawyers in welfare and in divorce work, are in a less oppressive job ghetto than teachers in elementary schools and librarians. And by opening some of the doors, they have made it possible for the younger professionals to branch out.

Nanette Dembitz, the first woman to run for judge on the New York State Court of Appeals, was a top scholar at the competitive Columbia Law School and editor of the *Columbia Law Review*, but instead of going into a big law firm or becoming secretary to a high-ranking judge —the usual next step for a *Columbia Law Review* editor— she went into labor law, then government employment, and later worked for the New York Civil Liberties Union and Legal Aid, before she was appointed a Family Court Judge.

Did she go into these areas because she was a woman and so more interested in the oppressed? Or did she take the jobs that were open to her? At this remove, it might be hard even for Judge Dembitz to answer honestly, but the moral for aspiring women and the tactic used by the women who succeed makes career sense: get ahead by finding a "woman's angle" to the work you want to do.

If there isn't one, manufacture it.

A woman with a masculine skill such as mathematics could also pursue the health, education, and welfare route, if she is not interested in pioneering. A woman statistician, for example, will be welcomed in health statistics, where there are many women professionals working as nurses, social workers, or therapists.

What kind of education work can a woman do in a male-dominated organization?

The possibilities are getting better all the time. More and more of the work in industry, government, and the professions involves training and retraining workers in new methods, and the newer and faster-changing the field is, the more teaching and training there is to be done.

Woman have nosed into the most masculine occupations as teachers. During World War II, the armed forces needed a great many weather forecasters. Because men were in short supply, the government gave a corps of women a crash course in meteorology and put them to work teaching aviation cadets. One of these trainers was Joanne Simpson, who now heads her own research group at the National Oceanic and Atmospheric Administration, formerly the U.S. Weather Bureau. She spent much of 1971 flying around and through thunderstorms from her base in Florida.

Do you want to get into security analysis, insurance, investment banking, carpentry, or foreign relations? Talk to women who have made it in these fields and you'll find that many of them started as trainers. And you'll find women training the men in some aspect of these traditionally male fields today.

The nice thing about "feminizing" a male job by

finding some way to teach it is that the industries that need a lot of trainers are the most forward-looking, expanding fields.

Computer companies need more trainers than shoe companies. Computers are mysterious and a great many people have to be taught how to make, sell, use, and repair them. Many of those who do the extensive training and teaching required are women. The career of Barbara Boyle is instructive. She went to work for IBM as a systems engineer, and moved from there to teaching salesmen. Her big leap into management occurred when she decided one day that if she could teach the salesmen how to sell, she ought to be able to do it herself. As it turned out, her biggest selling feat was to sell the IBM management on her own ability to sell. She worked up to marketing manager and assistant branch manager before quitting in 1972 to form her own consulting firm. As president of Boyle Kirkman Associates, Inc., Ms. Boyle is teaching again. Now her students are management executives learning how to utilize women employees, and women learning how to break into management.

Aerospace, the most forward-looking field of all, offers many opportunities for women because it has to teach so many different things to so many different kinds of people. The first woman to land on the moon is probably doing one of those training jobs now.

How does the welfare aspect of women's work open up new jobs?

The welfare "industry" today is so big, it involves so much money, and it is so political, that it has become man's work. The very way public welfare is now organized minimizes the one-to-one relationship between social worker and client that has always been considered women's work.

But even as women lose out in the welfare agencies, they find opportunities in the welfare emphasis that is reforming law, medicine, and even marketing and politics. Young lawyers and doctors have gravitated to legal aid, public health, and government jobs, the welfare end of law and medicine. Medicare, Medicaid, and the new comprehensive health service plans should create many more welfare-oriented jobs in which women will find ready acceptance.

Then there is consumerism, the welfare aspect of advertising and marketing. Big companies take seriously the new emphasis on car safety, pollution control, truth-in-advertising, and unit pricing.

To prove their sincerity, consumer-goods companies have been putting women in policy-making jobs. And women behavioral scientists have been active in developing "social indicators" to measure the well-being of our country in the way that "economic indicators" measure prosperity.

The *internal* welfare of a business or organization is also acceptable woman's work. Jobs in personnel, employee relations, and house-organ editing are frequently filled by women. These and other internal welfare functions tend to become more important as the organization grows larger and more impersonal.

I'm supposed to be good at getting along with people. Is this a feminine asset I can use to career advantage?

It certainly is—and managers are beginning to catch on to this fact. In banks, women officers are still rare, but in a survey for the First National City Bank of New York consultants found that the women rated significantly higher than the men in their desire to serve, and 11 percent higher in politeness and efficiency, the two traits that customers consider to be the most important.

The consulting firm of Cresap, McCormick, and Paget, Inc., recommended that women should be assigned to be "platform officers"—those who deal with the public—whenever possible.

Women are the traditional sympathizers, the traditional smoothers of human relations, and the bigger and more impersonal every aspect of our lives becomes, the more need for counselors, interviewers, communicators, liaison "men," adjusters, and that very new helper, the ombudsman representing individuals who feel lost in the vastness of a big company, a big university, or a big government agency. The ombudsman is a corporate welfare worker. The personnel department is a corporate wife and mother, concerned with internal relations and organizational morale. Both functions are expanding, and both provide growing opportunities for professional women.

Police work is putting more emphasis on human relations and less on the image of the policeman as a billy-swinging authority. That means greater acceptance for women on the force. Manufacturers are putting more emphasis on servicing their products and less on initial high-pressure selling. That means a need for more women to deal with unhappy customers.

Women are also taking over the formerly male job of school-bus driver. School administrators who have tried them like them because they get along better with the children than some of the male drivers. (The sex switch also says something about a change in attitude toward discipline.)

3

Nonsexist Career Opportunities

Will there be jobs available for women in the so-called male fields?

Yes, according to all the manpower forecasts. Janice Hedges, an economist with the Bureau of Labor Statistics, says "Many more women workers in the 1970s must prepare to enter work outside the traditional women's occupations if they are to find jobs in keeping with their abilities." Up till now, the growing numbers of working women in the total labor force have been crowded narrowly into women's fields, and those fields cannot continue to absorb all the women who may wish to enter the labor market in the future.

She advises women to go into the skilled trades, to become appliance servicemen, business-machine servicemen, automotive mechanics. In the professions, she suggests that women train to become doctors, dentists, or engineers.

For college graduates, the best opportunities will be in the male-dominated occupations, according to Herbert Bienstock, Middle Atlantic regional director of the Labor Department's Bureau of Labor Statistics. Occupations with an excellent outlook and more than 10,000 annual openings expected during the 1970s, include accounting, engineering, medical technology, medicine, and systems analysis, all primarily male now except for medical technology. Employment in the life sciences will also have a rapid growth through the 1970s, but according to the forecasters, "the number of life science graduates also is expected to increase rapidly and result in keen competition for the more desirable positions."

How can I find out whether a man's job is for me?

Because women have been restricted to "women's work," many of them have aptitudes that they have never discovered. Almost as many girls as boys are good at figures, for instance, but the girls lose this ability because so many of them are steered away from math.

A woman who doesn't know what she wants to do should take a battery of vocational aptitude tests. They are available to anyone free at most state-employment services, although you do have to ask for them. Vocational tests are sometimes available free or at a modest fee from the local YWCA. Private testing services may charge a steep price, but they sometimes offer highly skilled counseling and interpretation of the results. Facilities vary from community to community. In New York state, for instance, the Board of Cooperative Educational Services offers sophisticated testing and training for specific trades. The guidance counselor at the local high school should know what is available.

Vocational tests are of many different kinds. Some ask

you to do problems. Some set mechanical tasks. Most are paper-and-pencil tests of the true-false or "check one" variety that can be scored by machine.

Most people who take vocational-aptitude tests turn out to be fitted for a number of different vocations, some of which are apt to be a surprise. On one vocational-interest test, Marge Godfrey, the "exec" who coordinated the research for this book, turned out to have interests that most closely resembled those of officers in the U.S. Navy. The naval career did not appeal to her because she has a husband and disapproves strongly of anything connected with war. Such tests will broaden a woman's vocational horizons, but they can't always tell her what she ought to be doing. To be of any use, they must be interpreted and discussed with a guidance counselor.

How does a woman decide what male field would be best?

Joanne Simpson, a well-known meteorologist, believes that a woman should cold-bloodedly seek a field so underpopulated that employers are scraping the bottom of the barrel. That means watching manpower forecasts in the newspapers, writing to the government for pamphlets on occupation outlooks (see the resource section at the back of this book). Then she has to single out the area that is most suited to her talents. There may be a desperate shortage of statisticians, but if she can't balance a checkbook, and what's more, hates to do it, a job in statistics is not for her.

I've just finished high school, and I want to work. Can I earn a good living without a college degree?

A high-school graduate who doesn't want to go on

in school is able to earn $2 to $3 an hour as a retail clerk, or $2.25 an hour as a telephone operator, two occupations in which the employer pays for the small amount of training that is necessary. If she goes on to junior college, she may well wind up as a typist at $400 a month —hardly enough to warrant the expense and time of even "secretarial school" training.

She can do much better than that, however. Many women have mechanical aptitudes and interests and could make more money if they invested in craft training rather than in book learning. See chapter 9.

Isn't teaching a good field for women because there are so many jobs?

There won't be in the future. There are now more teachers than farmers in the United States—and like the farmers, their numbers will probably start to decrease as the present decline in numbers of school-age children continues. Many women have gone into teaching because it was almost the only thing available and then discovered that it was not for them. On the scholarly level, there wasn't much else they could do with their education until recently. A woman who called herself an economist, a zoologist, a historian, or an anthropologist had to teach her discipline on the college level. Forty-two percent of all professional women are teachers—and more than one-third of all female college students major in education.

During the next decade, opportunities in elementary education are expected to be favorable only in "urban ghettos, rural districts, and in geographic areas where teaching salaries are low," or for teachers who are trained to work with handicapped children, according to the Labor Department. Many students who are now preparing for elementary teaching as a career will have to look elsewhere for jobs.

At the high-school level, "the supply of secondary teachers will significantly exceed requirements," and in the colleges and universities, "new Ph.D.'s will face stronger competition for openings as their numbers grow each year." Other careers that appeal to college-educated women and have an excellent job outlook, such as city planning, occupational and school counseling, oceanography, and food science, are still so small that they can employ very few women.

What about the traditional fields for women college graduates other than teaching?

Nursing, which does need more people, will not be able to absorb all the women who won't be able to get jobs in teaching. Librarians were in great demand until very recently, but there has been a leveling off, and there will not be a great increase in the numbers needed. In social work, the demand will be there, but women are a declining proportion in this field.

Medical laboratory work is increasing, but more trained people are being turned out all the time, and manpower experts expect that the supply will fill the demand. It's the same story for home economists, nutritionists, and dieticians.

The Labor Department does not anticipate that the traditional women's professions will offer opportunities for all the women who are expected to get college degrees in the next decade. Unless a woman is prepared to fight very severe competition, and has a burning desire for one particular profession, she would do better outside the traditional job ghetto.

Don't women advance faster in one of the women's professions?

Some teachers, nurses, home economists, and social workers do say they've escaped discrimination because women dominate their work, and a few say they entered these fields for that reason. But now men are displacing women in these fields, or more accurately, the nature of the work is changing so that more of the work is in administration and policy-making, functions that are traditionally assigned to males, and less of the work involves direct contact with children, patients, or welfare clients. In social work, for instance, the new jobs are in community organizations, where the jobs have always been held by men, rather than in casework, traditionally done by women.

Then, too, as schools, hospitals, and welfare organizations grow, the job of heading them becomes big and well-paid enough to attract ambitious men. School superintendents and deans of home economics and social work schools are more frequently male, and the new males are often bitter about the "old girls" who resent being sidetracked. This is easy to see in the state of New York, where, in 1972, women comprised 57.6 percent of the professional educators in the state's public schools, but only 1.7 percent of high-school principals, and 2.6 percent of superintendents. Women teachers predominated in the elementary schools, but they held only 20.1 percent of the principalships.

I've always wanted to be a nurse. Now everyone says that nurses are underpaid, overworked, and mistreated by doctors, and I ought to be a doctor instead. Is nursing that bad?

It will always be the profession of choice for many women.

Actually, in 1971 the number of students enrolled in nursing schools increased significantly over enrollment in the previous years. When some entering students were interviewed in the *New York Times,* they made it clear that they see themselves as professionals with a different function from that of doctors. The women who are choosing the nursing profession today are motivated by a desire to provide continuous, primary care for patients. They do not see themselves as doctors' handmaidens.

Nursing pay has doubled in the last decade, and at the same time, nurses have been given more responsibility because there are so few of them.

I'd like to go to law school, but I'm not interested in practicing. Would such professional training be an asset to me in some other field?

Professional training is always an asset, and frequently it opens up areas that might otherwise be closed to a woman.

Florence V. Lucas, deputy commissioner of the New York State Division of Human Rights is a good example. The job does not require a law degree, and most of the men with whom she deals are laymen. But since the agency oversees the antidiscrimination laws, her sheepskin gives her special credibility. Professional training opens up doors to good jobs outside the field of study. Teachers are in demand for selling and research jobs. The first stewardesses were registered nurses, not because nursing was really needed in the air, but because their professional status was thought to command the respect of the passengers. This misuse of professional training is a waste to society, but it gives the individual woman the self-confidence that is seldom built into girls as they are growing up. Professional training is the easiest way for a woman to show that she is "twice as good."

Can a woman who wants a family fill all the requirements for training in a profession that is geared to men, such as medicine?

Yes, it can be done, given the proper encouragement and setting. Virginia Sadock, who went to medical school with the encouragement of her psychiatrist-husband, thinks that medical schools should plan curricula around the lives of married women students. She was lucky enough to get into a four-year residency program at the New York Medical College that was created for prospective doctors who are also prospective mothers.

In most medical schools and teaching hospitals, the woman has to scheme to fit her own pregnancy into the demanding schedule. Female students have been known to plan the arrival of the baby to coincide with duty on the pediatric ward so that they can keep an eye on their own child while on duty. Most schools regard themselves as big-hearted if they permit mother-students to take sick leave, or allow them to make up exams that they miss while giving birth. In the Metropolitan Hospital program, Dr. Sadock was able to work on a reduced schedule during the semester in which her baby was born. The tactic for getting around the masculinism of medical school, or any other institution, is to find one that is willing to adapt its structure to a woman's specific needs. The analog in an industrial setting would be structuring jobs so that mothers could work part time.

How important is professional training for a college graduate?

Obviously it would be hard to plead a case in the Supreme Court without special training, but in many fields of business the generally educated, or even those with no college at all, frequently do as well as those who go to professional schools. This is particularly true where salesmanship or individual talent is involved. Stacy Carter had made a name for herself as a saleswoman, first for a cosmetics firm, and then for Burlington Industries, where she sold fabrics for uniforms to manufacturers. One of her customers was the firm of David Crystal, Inc., and they were so impressed with her ability that she became a division manager for them when she was twenty-five, without a college degree and without any training in fashion.

Journalism is another profession relatively open to women, which takes and promotes the generally educated on an equal basis with journalism-school graduates. In these fields, talent is the determining factor.

Would further training help a college graduate who wants a business career?

A master's degree in business administration (M.B.A.) from Harvard, Pennsylvania (Wharton School of Finance), Columbia, or other highly rated school of business, is the quickest way to get on the business-management ladder. For highest salary, and equal pay with similarly educated males, a woman should choose a major leading to a growing field that is presently male-dominated. The big accounting firms and the burgeoning real-estate and land-development companies have competed most eagerly for the recent M.B.A.'s and they offered women graduates the same pay as men.

Do all the women M.B.A.'s receive the same fancy offers as the men?

Not quite. Bernardine Miller, placement officer for the University of Pennsylvania, notes that the 1972 male M.B.A.'s still commanded higher starting salaries than the women. The main reason was that the women averaged twenty-three years of age while the men, who typically entered the graduate school after a few years of business experience, averaged twenty-six.

The age gap is in itself evidence of sex discrimination. Male college graduates can get nonsecretarial jobs leading to promotion before they go for the master's degree, while the women who want careers in business have to go directly to graduate school and so they are younger than their male fellow students. In an effort to redress this imbalance, the Harvard Business School has a program to place women in business firms after they have been accepted for admission so that they can get the kind of practical experience that the male students have usually had.

What will be the best industries and companies for women in the future?

Highly paid jobs will open up for women first in financial services, banks, and insurance companies; second, in consumer products; third, in merchandising and retail business; fourth, in real estate, building, and construction; fifth, in entertainment and leisure time; and sixth, in the public sector. The forecast comes from executive recruiter Lester Korn; other experts concur that opportunities for women in finance will be widespread.

James Cleary, executive vice-president of Blyth Eastman Dillon & Company, whose firm employs women to sell securities, says that they are as capable as men as security analysts, and sometimes even better as investors.

The position of women in these areas as executives and professionals is already favorable in comparison with other fields. As far back as 1966, a study made by the Equal Employment Opportunity Commission of white-collar employment in one hundred major New York City companies showed that banking and insurance firms employed more women in highly paid jobs than all other industries except communications.

In the big corporations, opportunities should also be good in personnel, in marketing and sales, and in other departments where there have been few women, such as production, manufacturing, engineering, and general management.

Another good area for ambitious women will be in professional services—accounting, management consulting, executive recruiting. These consulting and business-service enterprises are usually small and depend directly on the talent and competence of individual professionals, which gives an exceptionally competent woman a chance to show her assets.

Are women more apt to get good jobs in one part of the country than another?

Both the East Coast and California have more highly placed women than the Midwest. New York, Washington, Atlanta, and Los Angeles are the places to go for a woman who really wants to get ahead.

The phone company always has lots of jobs for women. Isn't it better there than it used to be?

Because the phone company is one of the biggest

and most visible employers in the country, the Equal Employment Opportunity Commission (EEOC) investigated in depth its treatment of minorities and women employees and found much to criticize. As a result, in January 1973 the American Telephone and Telegraph Company agreed to give $15 million in back pay and $23 million in raises to women and minority males who were found to have suffered discrimination in job assignment, pay, and promotion. More than three-quarters of those getting back pay were women.

The phone company was a good target for such an investigation because it has always had so many women employees. It was the first to hire women in large numbers and adopted personnel policies intended to attract sheltered young women of good families whose parents would not have wanted them to work in factories or rough places. This meant that installations and repair, wiring, and outside jobs carrying higher pay and a chance to advance to management positions were always filled by men. Some years back, college-educated women were told they were "overqualified" because personnel officers felt that they quickly would become bored with the operator jobs to which females in the company were confined. Recently, however, the Bell System has been moving away from the idea that some jobs are for men, and others for women.

In 1972 the phone company agreed to place a specified number of women in the traditionally male craft jobs, and a specified number of men in traditionally female clerical and operator jobs. The agreement provided that women being moved into craft jobs would be awarded lump-sum damages for past exclusion, and those few already in the craft jobs were given back pay to bring them up to the level of the men who had entered the company at higher pay.

Someone suggested that I take a Civil Service exam—do women do better in the government?

The Federal government was the original equal-opportunity employer. Merit promotion regardless of race, creed, color, or sex has been the policy of the Federal Civil Service for fifty years. That does not mean, however, that the government has been immune from the general cultural bias against promoting women.

But don't Civil Service regulations protect women from discrimination?

Theoretically, yes. There is an elaborate grievance system with hearing examiners and even lawyers for civil servants who feel that they have been unfairly treated. But the system is so cumbersome that it is a formidable undertaking for a lower-grade employee to follow through on a complaint.

Grievance machinery for handling sex-discrimination cases has been strengthened by the formation of a Federal Women's Program that attempts to educate agency heads to utilize women better, and inform women employees about their job rights. Every Federal department now has to have an equal opportunity officer (EEO) watching over sex discrimination. The result has been a growing awareness of sex barriers and the need to overcome them.

A woman who feels she has a valid complaint should try to get the help of someone who knows her way around the Federal bureaucracy. Then she can discuss the problem with her EEO counselor, who will attempt to help her work out a solution informally.

If this doesn't work, she can file a formal written complaint with her EEO officer, who will start the investigative machinery. Sometimes this will lead to a hearing by the Civil Service Commission, and if that procedure is unsatisfactory, she then has the right to appeal to the courts.

I've read that President Nixon is doing a lot for women in Federal service. Is this just talk?

There have been splendid moves on paper. Women have been added to affirmative action programs to upgrade minorities, but it took several years for guidelines spelling out the procedures to be issued. Although personally conservative about the role of women, President Nixon gave moral support to equal opportunity in 1971 by directing Federal agencies to increase the number of women in top appointive positions. He subsequently named a few women to important posts, including Barbara Franklin, who was assigned the task of recruiting female talent for high-level government jobs.

I notice that the Civil Service gives preference to veterans. Doesn't this discriminate against women?

Yes, and this will be true until women are no longer discriminated against in the armed forces. If the Equal Rights Amendment is approved, such discrimination will be unconstitutional.

What kind of complaints about sex discrimination do Federal women make?

The most frequent complaint is that Federal service has different promotion ladders. Clerical workers without college training enter a clerical ladder that goes up only so far. We were told by one middle-level employee, "My advice to secretaries in the Federal service who do not wish to be secretaries is to quit and go do something else. There are two different categories in the Federal government. There is the clerical help, and there are professional people. The twain never meet."

Some feminists in the Federal government want the entire Civil Service classification standard for secretaries eliminated. They contend that it stifles the opportunity of secretaries because it ties their advancement to the rank of their bosses. "A secretary in the government can't hope to achieve on her own," one informant told us.

Meanwhile, college graduates are given a stiff examination and started on an entirely separate professional ladder that offers promotion to the higher-paying Civil Service grades. This means that some of the most experienced women, who have been secretaries for years, are stuck and can't get more money or a better title.

I've worked in the government for ten years, and I'm really doing the work of my boss. What can I do about it?

In the past, government women have broken through clerical and technical ceilings by the heroic device of dropping down in grade to get on the professional ladder. The problem has been that once a clerical or technical employee reaches the top grade in her classification, there is nowhere else to go. If she wants to move to professional classification, for which she may be qualified by experience or education, she has to move back to a lower grade—which invariably means a drop in pay.

Bette Krenzer, an electronics engineer at Wright-Patterson Air Force Base in Dayton, Ohio, is a good case in point. She got started during World War II as a technician, and returned to college at the end of the war when she was laid off. When she was rehired, it looked as if she would have to drop four grades to lower pay in order to get on the professional ladder to which her college training entitled her. A fair-minded boss helped her avoid this initial regression, but subsequent advancement took years of career time to accomplish.

And other professional women are still taking the low road to reach the high road. At Wright-Patterson, an editorial assistant rated G.S. 6 on the Civil Service scale, recently took a demotion to G.S. 5, in order to get into the training-level grade from which she could advance to a technical publications editor.

Is there any way for a government woman who wants to advance to get herself reclassified?

The Federal Women's Program and the U.S. Civil Service Commission are trying hard to provide escape hatches for women stuck on the clerical ladder.

There's a new program called Upward Mobility. Employees on a dead-end ladder can get off it and onto the professional ladder, presumably without taking the cut in pay and grade which many higher-grade government women have voluntarily taken to make the switch in the past. The program often involves government-sponsored training for the higher positions. There is a catch, though. A woman almost has to find a specific opening for the job she would like, before she will be allowed to get the training at government expense.

What happens to women when government programs are cut back?

Women and minorities get a chance to move up when organizations are expanding, and they can be in trouble during a RIF—which means "reduction in force." In a RIF, fewer jobs are available, and men want the jobs that women hold.

During the Nixon administration, RIF's have been more common than expansion. The better jobs to which a woman might aspire if she did get on the professional ladder have not been there, and other women are sometimes reorganized out of good jobs to make room for men.

When you're reorganized out of a job, can you find work in another government installation?

Open job posting is a goal of most affirmative action programs. A woman can find out where the jobs are posted in her area by contacting the person in charge of affirmative action in her department, a representative of the Federal Women's Program, or her EEO counselor.

Are there now opportunities for women in the armed forces?

Current military policy is to assign servicewomen to just about everything but combat duty. The United States has both women generals and admirals. West Point, Annapolis, and the Air Force Academy have been put on notice that they must prepare to accept women for training as future officers; and all the services are moving to correct policies that in the past gave the wives of servicemen more privileges in the Post Exchange, medical care, and other facilities than were extended to the husbands of the few married women in uniform. An effort has also been made to assign to the same posts married couples who are both in the service.

The Army, Navy, and Air Force always tried to recruit women volunteers for clerical work to cut down on the number of men who had to be drafted. There will be more women in uniform now that all who serve will be volunteers, because the pay and conditions that have to be offered make the armed forces an attractive alternative for some women. And when the Equal Rights Amendment is passed, any future draft will have to set up conditions for service that apply to women as well as men.

I'm a college girl who needs to make money in a hurry to pay back my college loan. What's the fastest way for me to make money?

Try jobs usually done by men. Ruth Steinberg, part-time receptionist for authors Eliot and Elizabeth Janeway, makes a minimum of $5 an hour as a bartender. She got started when she was a student at Barnard and took a course in bartending at Columbia. She soon discovered that she couldn't get jobs, as the other students were doing, through the university placement service because she was a woman, so she struck out on her own. Bartending at private parties is more profitable than catering, she says. She has had no trouble with men at parties, although they are curious, and "the market for bartenders is incredible!"

The classic way for college students to earn a lot of money fast is to work as a waitress, preferably at a resort hotel where room and board go with the job so that the salary and tips can be banked. Cocktail waitresses earn more than restaurant waitresses. The work is easier and the tips are higher—especially in supper clubs, where the indignity of an outrageous get-up must be endured.

Many blue-collar service jobs, such as driving a cab, a camp bus, or even a truck, enable a woman to earn money quickly without extensive training. Almost anything connected with construction pays higher than the going rate for women's jobs, including field paper work, such as timekeeping, which has been denied to women in the past because of the mystique that prescribes anything in building as a job for men only and because of the specious notion that a separate toilet must be provided for women in the field.

Some women college students take temporary advantage of special skills or aptitudes to earn money in fields that they do not wish to pursue as careers. In order to get out of debt, women college students have played in bands, modeled clothes, acted in television commercials, and taught everything from dancing to tennis.

I never went to college. Now I must return to work and earn money. Does lack of college training rule out high-paying jobs?

Absolutely not. Commission selling is open to anyone willing to take the risk, regardless of education, previous experience, or sex, and those who are good at it are among the highest wage-earners in the country. Turnover is high because many people try it, and then discover that they don't have the aptitude. There are always opportunities, and they are frequently better in fields that have had few or no women, like selling cars. According to Jon Duringer, the car dealer in Coronado, California, in 1972 there was a 30-percent shortage of sales personnel in General Motors dealerships throughout the country. That year he had seven women and eight men on his sales staff and some of the women earned more than some of the men.

There are many things that need to be sold, and the training is available at little or no cost, sometimes on the job. Women can and have been selling insurance, real estate, advertising space, and securities.

But it doesn't have to be selling. An increasing proportion of women in interesting high-paying work have simply plunged into a field that attracts them. Madelon Talley, who manages a Dreyfus fund, had dropped out of college to marry and when she went back to work, she started as a receptionist and general research worker, doing whatever came to hand, and learned the business very quickly. She also put herself through a rigorous training program—she says she cut out all social activities the first year she worked, and spent four or five hours reading material every night after dinner.

She regarded her whole employment as a learning experience. She took on all the chores that were around to do. As assistant to the boss she did all his letters, made his appointments, made his travel plans, and finally wound up supervising two secretaries. She also did a number of things that prevented her from being stuck in a subordinate job. First of all as assistant to the head of the outfit, she made the most of her opportunity to become known by men outside the organization who called the boss. She was careful to let them know that she was intelligent and knew what she was doing. This helped later on when she went into fund analysis on her own. She asked to be shifted from job to job so that she could learn more. When she asked for a new job, she saw to it that the job that she was doing did not suffer. Once, she realized that one of the new, young men in the office could do what she had been doing, and she physically switched offices with him. "What I did was to identify exactly what I was doing for the boss that needed replacing and then find someone who could do it for him," she explained.

Though in the past women may have been better educated than men doing their work, this may not be true in the future.

Suppose a woman does want to go back to school and get more training. How does she decide what courses to take?

She works backward and first decides what kind of job she wants. She should investigate the work available in her own company, and in her community. Libraries have a great deal of vocational-guidance material, and other sources of information are listed in the resource section at the back of this book.

When a woman knows what job she wants, or what field she wants to enter, she should find out what specific training is necessary to enter that field. Then, if she needs such training, she can go to the local community college, university, board of education, or whatever educational institution is most convenient. If they don't have the specific training that she needs, they may be able to suggest other places that provide it. And if she lives in an area that has very limited educational opportunities, she should investigate home-based, off-campus programs that are now offered by a number of institutions, and listed here in the resource section.

An educational program that is based on an employment goal is most likely to pay off, in money and in opportunity.

What about the courses advertised in the paper in computer programming, writing, art, motel management, or how to be a travel agent?

Many of these courses are not approved by any recognized educational authority, and some of them have been outright frauds. Before signing up, a prospective student should find out what the local education department knows about the course. Most important is the school's ability to provide jobs. It pays to find out how many of the graduates have been placed and are working in the field, and to talk to some of them about the course itself. Some of the most attractive fields, such as travel and motel management, are very small. The *Occupational Outlook Handbook,* available at most public libraries, lists the job possibilities in each of these fields and gives straightforward advice about how to get into them.

What if you aren't sure what you want to do with your life? Does it pay to knock yourself out on a job you may leave to rear a family?

By all means, yes. One of the women we interviewed puts it this way, "A job may not be a lifelong commitment, but you can be as dedicated during your working life as a dedicated man." What distinguishes the successful woman is not whether she quits to have babies or not, but whether she approaches whatever job she has as a learning experience.

Some career women have been concerned with the disservice a lackadaisical woman does to other, and presumably more dedicated women. But the biggest disservice involved is what she does to her own future options —after she has had her babies or in the next town to

which her husband is transferred, if temporary residency
is the reason for her lack of commitment.

*When my baby is born, I expect to stay home for a few years but
I'd like to keep up with my field so that I won't be too far behind
when I return to work. Do you have any suggestions?*

An enlightened employer who is knowledgeable
about the new management techniques, might think
about restructuring the work. Mary Estill Buchanan, the
management consultant, suggests that employees can be
assigned one-shot, single-problem assignments, or
short-term tasks that can be completed on a part-time
basis. A woman with specialized knowledge would do
well to enlist her employer's aid in setting up such a
program.

Academic women frequently make use of the baby-
tending years to do long jobs of research at home.
Professional women can keep in touch with their fields
by reading journals, attending meetings, and even by
arranging to see former colleagues periodically for a
catch-up lunch. A woman who has had a baby need not
lie fallow professionally.

*I am forty. Does it pay to go back to college or graduate school
to start a new career?*

It's best to have a specific goal in mind. Florence
Gaynor had left nursing to raise a family. She went back
to school to get a master's degree in public health administration. After graduation, she became coordinator
at the Albert Einstein College of Medicine and then
worked at Lincoln Hospital, where she was promoted to
assistant hospital administrator, and then rose to be-

come associate executive director. Like many successful
women, she learned to work with budgets and finance,
and eventually was appointed administrator of the Mart-
land Hospital, the teaching hospital of the New Jersey
Medical School College of Medicine and Dentistry, and
the largest hospital in New Jersey. She was the first
woman to hold such a job.

*Can a woman start an important career after her children are
grown?*

While it's better to start young, it is less of a handicap for women to start later than it is for a man because
women's career lines are less conventional. They aren't
on the ladder that moves up and out to begin with, so
they have less to lose by a late start.

A great many rather spectacularly successful women
started their careers after their children were grown.
That's what Madelon Talley did. She went to work at
thirty-six, as a receptionist and general researcher for the
head of the Dreyfus Corporation. Four years later she
was president of the Dreyfus Offshore Trust, the first
woman president of an investment fund.

Julia Walsh, the Washington, D.C., stockbroker who
was a pioneer woman member of the American Stock
Exchange, didn't start her career until she was widowed
with four children. There is an old adage in the personnel business: "It's not the age, it's the condition." And
companies are beginning to give serious consideration
to off-the-job equivalent experience, according to management consultant Mary Estill Buchanan. She contends
that many older women have learned through living
what men are sent to management training courses to
learn.

Beverly Pearson was admitted to the bar in 1950, and started to practice on her own so that she could fit it in with having children. But her husband's job took her to South America and Africa from 1955 to 1965. Her experience there was no help back home in Washington, D.C., when she opened a new law office.

What had changed, however, was the climate for women lawyers. She found it easier to get started in 1965, and the years in South America yielded an unexpected bonus by opening the door to Spanish-speaking clients who needed a lawyer who could communicate with them.

I haven't been working for a number of years. Is there any place I can turn for help in brushing up, finding out where I could work, and generally getting back into the job market?

A modest but comfortable industry has developed to recondition mothers—to encourage them to resume, or start specialized training, to help them sort out their psyches about whether they really are career oriented. The principal value of this advice, as its purveyors are the first to admit, is to build a woman's confidence. If she thinks she needs it, she probably does.

Continuing education courses for women offered at most colleges and universities have been attempting to meet the needs of women who have been full-time homemakers and want to step out. Business schools offer brush-up courses in typing and shorthand for those who must go back to this ghetto work, and there are aptitude-test organizations that give paper and pencil tests and try to match a woman's interests with occupations.

In the resource section of this book, there are lists of books to read for the woman who doesn't know where to begin, and names and addresses of organizations that offer special counseling, vocational analysis, training courses, workshops, and employment placement.

Many advisers to women returning to work think that any job, or even volunteer work, builds confidence in itself. If a woman can't afford the time or the money for special training or coaching, she can try a job that she is sure that she can do for a few weeks or months. An employment service that specializes in placing "temporaries" provides opportunities to get a taste of different fields and industries.

I haven't worked at a paid job for twenty years, but I've done all kinds of volunteer work in my community. Now I need income. What can I do?

Many women have been able to cash in on their years of volunteering. Frances Goldman, president of Distaffers Inc., an agency that specializes in the placement of professional women who have been out of the work force, says that frequently employers look more favorably on responsible volunteer work than they do on college credits. She thinks volunteer work is so valuable that she advises women who want to go back to work to do some volunteering as a first step.

To make the most of her volunteer experience, a woman should look for a paid job that has direct relevance to what she has been doing. Women who have been active in community-service work, for example, often find they can translate their skills into politics or government employment.

Frances Dias is a regional director for the Defense Civil Preparedness Agency, the first and only woman to hold this job. The agency works with local jurisdictions to assess their preparedness for national disasters or bomb threats. Her volunteer work in local government had given her special qualifications. Ms. Dias had served as unpaid councilman and mayor in Palo Alto, California. In local politics, salaries often are low or nonexistent, and the result, she says, "is that the men seek it [these jobs] because of prestige" and the women for service. While a housewife, she was the first mayor of Palo Alto to keep regular office hours and work full time. Because she spent time digging for answers, she could demonstrate to the doubting men that she was willing to offer "ideas without any credit to myself," and was able to gain valuable experience. When she subsequently sought paid employment, she was qualified to become an administrative assistant to a Congressman.

This job involved what she had already done: listening to people, looking into local situations, solving problems, and hearing complaints—and it led to her present appointment.

Antonina P. Uccello, the first woman mayor of Hartford, Connecticut, had done a great deal of volunteer work with local organizations while she worked at a local department store. She was elected to the city council while still employed. After her service as mayor of Hartford, she was appointed director of consumer affairs in the U.S. Department of Transportation.

Are there any special tricks to making volunteer work pay off?

Yes. A volunteer should join every organization that she can and become an officer if possible. Joining organizations outside, as well as inside, her field will put her in contact with potential employers.

Frances Dias finessed the job as volunteer mayor into

a well-paid appointment in the Nixon administration by making herself known outside Palo Alto. She went to the meetings of the Association of Mayors, the League of California Cities, and the U.S. Conference of Mayors.

When it comes time to evaluate unpaid work in terms of paid employment, it should be phrased in terms of the qualifications for a job. Ms. Dias could point to her contacts with city officials, and her detailed knowledge of city governments, qualifications that had readied her for the agency job.

I've been working with our town planning board and it's been fascinating, but I'm not likely to run for political office. Any other possibilities?

Urban planning has attracted many civic-minded women. It's a small field but new, which means that jobs are not rigidly defined or sex typed.

Practical skills such as drafting may be extremely helpful in getting one's foot in the door, according to Barbara Crosser, first woman on the staff of the planning department of the city of Joliet, Illinois. She was hired as the department's first woman draftsman in 1970, because of the experience she had with drafting tools while earning her master's degree in geography. She was soon doing extended studies under that title and when funds for a second draftsman were voted, moved ahead to the title of planner. The second draftsman was also a woman.

Some employment opportunities do exist with state, local, and federal government agencies, developers, research organizations, and urban planning firms that may be flexible about working hours for qualified women.

Edith Litt, now a vice-president with Raymond, Parish

and Pine, an urban planning firm in White Plains, New York, started with them on a part-time basis when her children were small.

I'd like to return to work. I was a good typist and never minded doing it. Is there still typing work available?

The demand for typists and stenographers has grown along with higher volumes of business, in spite of mechanization. Clerical work has not been computerized nearly as fast as the computer companies promised. Word processing, an assembly-line approach to stenographic work, is still in the future for most employers. Typing is a particularly good bet for a woman who only wants to work part time and it offers a way of getting back in the labor force, while investigating career possibilities.

A woman who has been confined to typing for too long should look at the suggestions later on in this book for getting out of the typing pool and onto the promotional ladder.

What about part-time work? I don't want to work a nine-to-five day as long as my children are too young to look after themselves after school. How much can I earn without working full time?

A woman has to take a whopping discount in pay per hour for the freedom to work when and as she pleases. Big users of routine clerical services, such as the subscription departments of national magazines and mail-order houses, often organize their work so that it can be done part time, and then they can tap the talent bargain of literate housewives who don't want to work a whole day.

This is not exploitative providing both sides to the

bargain know what they are doing. A woman who wants to work part time should compare the rate of pay she gets with that of full-time workers who have the same skills. Then she will know how much she is sacrificing per hour for freedom.

Work that is part time at the discretion of the employer is another story. It often carries premium pay. By asking around, a woman can sometimes find a situation in which the hours she wants to work coincide with the hours an employer needs—a job as receptionist during a doctor's office hours, for example.

4

Tactics for Job-Hunters: Predicting Discrimination

I'm about to look for a job. Do employment agencies tend to discriminate against women?

It's illegal, but in a 1973 survey, four out of five employment agencies accepted job orders from employers that specified men. Neal Hoffman, regional director of the New York State Division of Human Rights, lists some of the discriminatory practices he has observed:

Applications for men and women are different in color.

Applications for men and women have different questions.

Applications for women require data about secretarial skills; those for men do not.

Fees—and the length of time necessary to pay them —are different for men and women.

A woman can find out whether any of these games is being played by asking if applications are generally filed by job or by sex; and if by job, whether they are then filed alphabetically without regard to sex.

The employment agency told me that I would have to take a typing test, even though I'm not interested in a clerical job. Should I have agreed to do so?

No. It undoubtedly indicates that they refer women primarily to clerical jobs. Though it is now illegal for agencies to require tests of women that they do not require of men, it will be some time before they all catch up.

Are there employment agencies that don't send all women out on typing jobs?

Yes, there are some agencies like Distaffers, Inc., of Philadelphia that specialize in placing professional women, and they work very hard at maintaining that image. According to Frances Goldman, president of Distaffers, "We don't exclude nonprofessional jobs just to be snobbish; we want to very carefully maintain a professional image for the women we represent and are very aware that if we place secretaries as well as editors, many women with advanced degrees and good working experience would be offered typing jobs. And that's a bag we want to stay away from."

If an agency asks whether a woman has children, and doesn't ask men the same question, would this indicate that the agency is discriminatory?

Yes. It is now illegal to consider prospective employees who are mothers on a different basis from those who are fathers. An employment agency that asks a woman about her arrangements for the care of her children while she works has to be careful to ask a man the same question.

Are agencies the only way to get a job?

They are only one way, and the books on job hunting listed in the resource section of this book, cover all the other possibilities.

Many veteran employers say that the best applicants come from friends of present employees. So let your friends know of your interests; they will be able to tell you about conditions at their place, and they can be good letter boxes for relaying information about the job to you, and about you to the job.

Another approach that works well, particularly for a woman with a taste for adventure, is to advertise oneself. Suzanne Douglas, national sales manager of the *Ladies' Home Journal*'s Prime Showcase (an upper demographic edition) was stuck in secretarial work in California, and found it impossible to use her skills as a bridge to something better there. She ran a "situation wanted" ad in the *New York Times* that read:

MR. EXECUTIVE: NEWCOMER SEEKS CHALLENGING MANHATTAN CAREER. Sharp, efficient, discreet, personable, experienced, energetic, creative, young, and unencumbered GORGEOUS California lass. Arriving FUN CITY mid-June. College plus 9 years exp. as Exec/Pri/Soc/Legal Secy. & Admin. Asst. (Also Fashion Model). EXPENSIVE? Certainly. Box——.

She ran the ad just once, and got fourteen replies. At least three of them were worth investigating. The job she took involved managing several business enterprises for a busy company president, and she eventually became public relations manager of his main electronics company.

In that capacity, she encountered space salesmen who were soliciting her advertising business. She decided she could do their job better than they were doing it. Agencies specializing in placement of media representatives told her there wasn't a chance for a woman but she kept looking through friends of friends, and finally did locate a publisher's sales representative who was willing to "take a chance" on a woman. The ad had not only launched her in New York City, but led her into a new, and ultimately profitable, career.

How can I tell if my company or the company I would like to work for gives women a fair shake?

Ask questions, and look around. Here's a checklist of things to watch for. If the answers are not readily available, ask the personnel department.

Does every employment title or department in the organization include workers of both sexes? Are there any areas of the plant that are off limits to women?

Do any women supervise men? When jobs become available, are they openly posted so that everyone will know about them? Are all candidates formally evaluated in writing?

Are training or development programs open to women? Are there any women in them now? Does the company reimburse tuition for job-related night courses? Is there an affirmative action program?

Are medical insurance, pension plans, sick leave, and

overtime provisions the same for men and women? Is the company's maternity policy the same as for any other disability?

Here are some danger signs:

Company stag affairs that exclude women, such as dinners, lunches, clambakes, bowling teams, and golf days.

A tendency by company representatives to use language that is offensive to women (broad, girl, chick).

More attractive women seem to be put out front so as to give a sexier appearance.

A lot of gossip about office sex games.

Questions about an applicant's personal life, her marital intentions, her family plans.

A woman should be wary if the company's "help wanted" ads imply that the jobs are more suited to one sex or the other; if the company advertises in segregated columns in the newspapers; if it seems to be harder for women to apply than men.

How can I tell if this company is really interested in placing women in top management?

Check the preceding list, and then add:

Is there an officer or partner who is a woman? If not, does the highest-ranking woman report directly to the chief executive officer?

Does the highest-paid woman earn as much or more than a man at her grade level?

Has a woman replaced a man at a supervisory level during the past year?

Do women employees travel?

Are women reimbursed for membership in professional associations? Are women sent to industry conferences and meetings?

If a professional or technical woman had maternity

leave, did she return to work without a loss of seniority?

Does the management-training program include women? Is it open to mature women with solid experience and to those returning to business careers as well as to recent college graduates?

If the company recruits at colleges, do their recruiters include visits to women's colleges, and do they see both men and women candidates at coed schools?

When I'm applying for a job, how can I tell whether it could lead to promotion?

There are several good ways. Ask what happened to the person who previously held the job. Was she (or he) promoted? Fired? Or did the person quit? How long was the previous person in the job? What you hope to hear, of course, is that your predecessor was promoted. If she (he) quit, what about the person who held the job before her (him)?

Another question to ask: "If I accept this job, what position can I expect to advance to after two years, or after five years?"

Patricia Haskell, a former officer of the American Management Association, suggests that you say that you would hope to do a good enough job to merit promotion into an even more challenging job, and would consider it your professional responsibility to train someone to take your place. If this falls with a dull thud, you know that promotion was not in your potential employer's plans. Jane Kay, manager of employee relations for Detroit Edison, feels that those responsible for hiring should always give applicants an opportunity to state what they want to accomplish on the job, or in the future. That's the time, she suggests, to make it known that you would like to move ahead, and that you are willing to take on increased responsibilities.

Ms. Kay also thinks that a woman can learn a lot from a frank discussion of opportunities for women. "Nervous hedging or a flat statement by the interviewer that women have always been given the same opportunity as men would give me cause to wonder about the employer's sincerity," she says. On the other hand, chances for promotion are good if an employer sincerely wants to know about a candidate's aspirations.

I'm just out of college and looking for a job in business. What do I do first?

Plan a campaign before graduation, advises consultant Barbara Boyle. A graduating student should list general areas of interest that could be explored, such as accounting, market research, sales, or finance, to pinpoint specific jobs.

Next, she should write to leading companies that would have such jobs and ask them for appointments. She should explain in her letter that even if they do not have a job open, she would like to find out what kind of work goes on in their company.

Most major corporations are willing to talk to potential candidates, and employers do like to explain their work to young people. The exploratory interview offers a good chance to find out more about the duties and responsibilities of specific jobs, what people in these jobs do all day long.

The candidate should also ask what kind of ability, experience, or training is necessary, what is required for success, and what the job leads to.

Above all, the job hunter should not jump to conclusions about industries without detailed investigation. She should not assume that banking is dull, or that she doesn't want to be a manager. She should not think in stereotypes, nor look only for a glamour-type job.

It is also helpful to role-play the interview with friends ahead of time, so that the questions most likely to be asked will be familiar—good advice for anyone applying for a job at any time.

Can a beginner make enough in glamour jobs to live on?

So many recent college graduates want to get into publishing, radio, television, and some of the glamour fashion industries that the companies can hire superior talent for less than a competent secretary commands in other fields. This is all right if the jobs are in fact stepping-stones, apprentice jobs leading to promotion. But before a beginner takes such a job, she should inquire what has happened to the previous incumbents. Many of these glamour industries count on a high turnover of newcomers to get a great deal of routine work done very cheaply. The number of good jobs in any of these fields is so small that the promotion ladder is very steep.

Do personnel departments try to help women who don't want a woman's ghetto job?

Their past record has not been good. Many women are as bitter about the personnel departments they have had to fight for assignment to jobs with a future, as many of them are against their high-school guidance counselors who tried to steer them into "women's work."

Complaints are centered on the initial job interviews, when the interviewers tend to steer young women into secretarial and clerical jobs, and do not know enough about the operations of the organization to know whether or where there are promotional opportunities. Young women identify the personnel department as an outpost of the sexist establishment, and of course it usually is—even when, and especially when, it is headed by an older career woman who has worked her way up as a "woman's woman" riding herd on a large female ghetto.

Like vocational-guidance counselors, personnel-department interviewers are very frankly concerned with the odds or the main chances and have to deal in stereotypes. One economist says that the cost of getting enough information about or from an applicant to determine whether the stereotype does not apply may well exceed the value of a better job fit.

From the employer's point of view, losing a good candidate because of prejudice is not as serious as spending more money than is needed to take in a satisfactory low-level worker. As most jobs are low-level, and the work of most personnel departments is to keep all these high-turnover, low-level jobs filled, personnel workers have a natural tendency to shy away from the "over-qualified" and go by their own prejudices.

As in so much else in the employment picture, new laws will eventually make a difference here too. But until enforcement and compliance are widespread, a woman going in for her first job might have an experience like the one satirized in this skit, developed by the Quaker Oats Company of Chicago for presentation in its Equal Employment Opportunity Management Workshop:

An applicant named George is talking to the personnel department. After revealing that he majored in biochemistry, and is interested in a business career, he's asked about his typing speed. Then, the personnel interviewer begins to probe into George's personal life:

CHARLENE (the personnel interviewer): George, I see you're single.

GEORGE: Yes, I am.

CHARLENE: My goodness, I bet a young attractive man like you has a girlfriend . . .

George admits to dating, and under prodding, says "Naturally, I'd like to get married someday."

When the head of the department to whom he is referred elicits the same information, she reports back to Charlene: " . . . his typing isn't really good, and he's pretty serious about some girl. About the time we get him trained, he'll probably get married. Frankly, I think he's a poor risk."

Two disastrous interviews later, George finally catches on and says emphatically, "I've never been one for dating, and as for marriage, I'll probably be so busy with my career that I won't have time for any of that." But this approach doesn't work any better—the final interviewer reports back to personnel, "I can spot that type a mile away . . . they leave before you know it, and you never hear from them again. I wouldn't touch him with a ten-foot pole."

Should I tell them that I believe in equal opportunity for women when I apply for a job?

Equal opportunity is the law, so the subject should not come up at all. The interviewer has no right to ask about your personal opinions, or your membership in the National Organization for Women. If you volunteer the information, you can be accused of leading with your chin if you proclaim your militance, or being unfair to women activists who have improved your lot if you go out of your way to dissociate yourself from them.

I am a lesbian, and don't mind having sympathetic people know it, but will coming out of the closet keep me from getting a good job?

The topic seldom comes up in interviews because it is embarrassing and probably illegal to ask. After she is hired, a lesbian with guts can profit by saying to her employer, "It can't make any difference on the job, but I think you should know that I am not sexually attracted to men." This eliminates her supposed vulnerability to blackmail, and shifts the moral grounds from the sex habits of the employee to the employment criteria of the employer.

Supposing I don't want to set the world on fire. Should I pretend that I do to get the job?

On the contrary, in this sexist society, your "realistic" aspiration level is an asset. One personnel consultant advises employers that a woman with limited aspiration "may be much more profitable than one looking for administrative berths she can't possibly hope to fill." She tells interviewers to consider where the company would like to see the applicant in ten to twenty years if she is hired. Most of the time, it's right in the same entry job. She warns employers to beware the woman who wants "self-fulfillment" because it might mean "outdoing the man in the family or a man on the job."

I don't agree, but enough employers do to make it quite unnecessary to fake aspiration you don't have.

I interviewed for a job I'm sure I can do but the final verdict was that I wasn't qualified for it. What do you think I could have done to get the job?

Employment specialists say that women have more trouble than men in relating their experience to the particular job for which they are applying. Women must make a special effort to interpret what they have done because their experience is less apt to be in the conventional jobs the interviewer expects an applicant to have had.

If, however, a woman suspects that the interviewer is unconsciously biased, she can sometimes help him to see this by asking, in a friendly way, what credentials *could* have qualified her. If the interviewer tries to be explicit, he may discover that he really doesn't think that *any* woman is qualified to do the job.

What can you do if the qualifications the interviewer sets up are clearly unrelated to the job?

Manpower specialists privately agree that employers have become accustomed to demanding higher qualifications for many jobs than are really necessary. There's no reason, for instance, why a secretary needs a college education. You can't be an air-line pilot without special training, of course, but the more desirable the job, the more it depends on vague qualities such as "leadership" or "charisma," which defy definition, let alone testing.

Leonard Sayles, a professor at the Columbia Graduate School of Business, and author of a widely used text on personnel, says that it is especially hard for blacks and women to get management jobs because it is so hard to measure performance in advance (or even after the fact), that employers have to go on "mystique" or clutch at straws, such as appearance or college education. He points out that the hesitation to put a woman in a management job may only reflect the insecurity of the employer, who feels that it's safer to promote a person who is like the other people who have done the job. It was easier to ignore Jackie Robinson's black skin when he was being considered for a baseball team, where what counts is an objective, easily measured performance such as a batting average than when he was being considered for an executive job, where no one really knows how and whether anyone will score.

What about arbitrary qualifications? Can the police department refuse to hire me because I'm not tall enough?

Police departments have always had height and weight requirements for patrolmen that rule out most women applicants, on the unproven assumption that height commands respect from the public. Now the assumption is being challenged.

Now the Department of Justice bars height minimums for Federally funded law-enforcement officials on the grounds that such height requirements are discriminatory against women and Spanish-surnamed Americans, who tend to be shorter in stature than other men, and the State University of New York was forced to abandon a height requirement that disqualified most women applicants for the job of campus guard. It was agreed that a guard didn't have to be 5 feet, 7 inches tall to perform effectively.

At first glance, a height requirement seems to be fair because it applies to men and women alike, but the limitation actually favors men because more men than women are tall. Regulatory commissions are moving away from the notion that it is necessary to prove that the employer intended to discriminate and toward the idea that a qualification set up in good faith can be discriminatory if it is actually irrelevant to the job and has an "adverse impact" on a class of applicants.

If a qualification is demanded that seems clearly unrelated to the job, a woman might inquire why it is required. If she doesn't sound as if she were going to cause trouble about it, it just might get her the job!

However, the employer may have valid legal reasons for refusing to make any exception. If the job calls for specific training, and he decides to accept one candidate who does not have that training, he is inviting a charge of discrimination from any subsequent applicant who is turned down because of lack of training. A qualification that is not applied equally to everyone becomes suspect. Qualifications have been under attack by many people for many reasons, and have been defended with equal vigor by those who establish them.

When I applied for an outdoor sales job they gave me an aptitude test. I know I can do the job, but I'm not sure I passed the test —it was obviously designed for men. Is there anything I could have done?

Tests that discriminate against whole classes of applicants, such as blacks or women, are illegal both under the Civil Rights Act of 1964 and the executive orders barring discrimination in employment of government contractors and the Federal service. In order to be legal, the test must be based on some clear evidence that the scores are related to performance on the job for which they are given, and the population on whom the test is validated, or tested, must include blacks, women, and other minorities. Since few blacks or women have been allowed to work in many jobs, this requirement is very hard to meet, so that most of the employment tests being given could be challenged. According to a Chicago testing specialist, William Karp, of William Karp Consulting Company, Inc., a test is suspicious if it rules out all blacks and women who take it. Faced with such a test, a black or a woman might consider doing what white men have always done when the cards are stacked against them: figure out how to beat it.

In the appendix to *The Organization Man,* a pioneer attack on the inhumanity of life in the big bureaucracies, author William H. Whyte told his readers what to do on psychological tests. Try to decide, he says, exactly what kind of person you think the tester wants you to be and answer the way that person would. Back in 1957, Whyte suggested that a testee repeat to himself over and over, "I love my father and my mother, but my father a little bit more. I like things pretty well the way they are. I never worry much about anything. I don't care for books or music much. I love my wife and children, but I don't let them get in the way of company work."

That same advice works fine to this day for women, except, of course, that it's your husband you love without letting him get in the way of company work.

What do you say if an employment interviewer says you are "overqualified" for the job?

In the past, ambitious women have taken this put-off as a cue to go elsewhere. But recent laws and decisions assuring women equal opportunity have created a climate in which interviewers are more apt to anticipate the retort: Would a man with her credentials be dismissed as "overqualified"?

The challenge is legitimate, but the interviewer can't

change the system, and as a professional personnel specialist, is apt to see the inequity, not to say illegality, of the rules more clearly than his bosses. One personnel specialist who works for a big bureaucracy suggests replying with a more constructive question: "All right, then, what job do you have that my higher qualifications would make me eligible for?" If there is none, then the way is open for her to explore further with the interviewer her reasons for wanting a job that is supposedly beneath her, and the interviewer's concern about giving it to her.

Some of the questions in the interviewer's mind might be: Will this overqualified applicant be happy in the kind of job we need filled? Will she stay long enough to repay the cost of training her? Is turnover a special problem in the department in which she will be working? Will she become a morale problem? Why is she willing to take this job?

Manpower specialists say that no employer really knows how much turnover costs, but no one likes to hire a person who looks obviously temporary if the job takes more than a half day's training.

What do you do when you can't find a job for which you have had training and you suspect it is because you are a woman?

It can happen to any woman, whether she is a mechanic or a new Ph.D. She has to explore every avenue, complain to everyone involved in the training process, to her school, to her state's human rights commission, to the state employment agency—anything that suggests itself. Janie Cottrell, who had been trained as a welder, had to take a job she didn't like because it involved paper work (she went into welding in the first place because she didn't like office work). Finally she placed a telephone call to the governor of her state of Georgia. Although she didn't get the governor himself on the phone, an aide alerted the state employment service, and in no time she was hired as a welder at Scientific-Atlanta, Inc.

A woman scientist who had encountered no discrimination in graduate school, couldn't get a job after she got her Ph.D. She went to the head of her department, and to the president of the university, and told them she thought they ought to take as much responsibility for placing her as they do for placing their male Ph.D.'s. They agreed and found an assistant professorship for her. "Don't let the department which awarded your degree forget their responsibility," she advises. "Your failure is their failure."

I don't believe that sex makes that much difference, so what do I say when a prospective employer tells me he has to have a woman for the job?

A woman who is hired *because* she is a woman owes it to herself to find out why—especially if it's a good job that has previously gone to a man. During the economic slowdown of 1970 and 1971, women college graduates were hired by many employers for the first time. Before the slowdown, business was expanding, and those entry jobs were used for training future male executives. Where prospects for promotion are less favorable because of economic conditions, an employer may look for someone who will be content to do a routine job forever. Or there may be something wrong with the working conditions of the job that a man wouldn't tolerate.

Women are sometimes hired because they are supposed to be more patient in handling complaints.

If the job is poorly designed, so that its authority is unclear, a docile woman who won't demand a clarification may look like the cheapest and easiest solution.

The owner of a small business may put a woman in charge because he feels that she won't challenge policies or exceed her authority.

If there is a conflict within the organization, a woman may be put in a sensitive spot simply because she doesn't look as if she would rock the boat.

In small organizations, a woman may be preferred because she is a talent bargain who will turn in more performance per dollar of salary than a less talented male.

Sexist reasons for preferring a woman may not be flattering, but many successful women—perhaps the majority—have swallowed their pride and turned the put-downs to career advantage. There's nothing wrong with an ambitious young woman taking such a job, providing that she and her employer both understand that she regards the job as a stepping-stone and may not stay after she has learned what it can teach her.

Some reasons for preferring a woman may be so personal that they don't show up until the woman is in the job. "Watch out for any man who is out to hire a woman specifically—either he's a lech or an alcoholic," Monica de Hellerman, vice-president of Bass & Company, a financial public relations firm, warns on the basis of her observations of many different kinds of organizations. "The alcoholic usually takes on a bright woman to take over while he's out drinking, but thinks that she will pose no threat to his job."

In the 1970s, the most common reason for preferring a woman is to show that the organization is sincerely trying to comply with equal opportunity laws and executive orders.

When I apply for a job, should I tell them I know how to type?

Let's face up to this one directly. Many women boast that they purposely never learned to type, and if they did learn, they won't admit it. Others, like Jane Johnson, for years manager of Vassar's Vocational Bureau, have advised women to learn typing—on the ground that it's a skill that everyone should learn—but not shorthand.

The successful women we interviewed had no one answer. Lillian Lynch, general supervisor of Illinois Bell's human resources staff, says that she did not study typing and shorthand so that she would not be automatically cast as a secretary.

A woman administrator in the Department of Agriculture also says no on the matter of typing. "If you are a secretary, that's your image forever," she says. She herself has never admitted she could type. If asked, she just says she doesn't do it very well.

Pamela Ilott, now a television producer, was willing to do almost anything, including scrubbing floors, to avoid clerical work. "If I had known how to type, I would have become the office manager," she says. A former English actress, she got her start when she offered to tutor, for free, the children of a man who had a broadcasting rights firm, if he would give her a professional job. She promised she would learn in a week to do something for the money they paid her or quit. He gave her a try and she stayed.

Pat Pepin, now executive director of Country Living Associates, a real-estate company, used her secretarial skills to get a job three or four times in her career. But she still says she would not advise a girl to learn shorthand and typing, "especially in New York where there are many other opportunities." If a woman can't type and do shorthand, she is *forced* to look outside the ghetto. She can't fall back on a woman's job.

The argument is as old as the female ghetto itself. Back when I was a little girl, the ghetto was the kitchen, and women were telling their daughters, "Don't learn to cook and you'll never have to do it." The implication was that their daughters should sell themselves (it sounds like literal prostitution) to some man rich enough to support a cook. Of course, most girls had to learn to cook anyway but if they wished they could use their awkwardness in the kitchen to reinforce the reproach "My mother never raised me to slave in a kitchen" and spur their husbands to earn more.

The argument against learning anything is just as self-defeating, I believe, in the office. It's not knowing how to do something that sticks you with the dull job.

For many women who work in fields where writing is important, such as publishing and advertising, typing is a necessary tool. A woman who has a clearly earmarked career goal may need to type to get started in that field. Joanne Simpson, the pioneer meteorologist we interviewed, says every ambitious woman should learn to type, and to teach, and to do both of these well.

Letty Pogrebin, author of *How to Make It in a Man's World*, hedges a little bit, and says that a woman looking for a job in the corporate world should type well enough to pass the typing test in a job interview, but she shouldn't claim to be a speed demon, or they will surely try to bury her behind the machine.

Joan Abrams, the superintendent of schools in Montvale, New Jersey, has stopped typing since she has been promoted to the top because she feels it is inappropriate. She doesn't think a professional woman should type, although she did her own typing when she was on the way up.

5

Tactics for Promotion:
Avoiding Discrimination

Does it ever pay to take a secretarial job?

Yes, of course. Many successful women have found secretarial jobs to be a good jumping-off point. And since there are more than 3 million secretaries and stenographers, there are lots of jobs available. But because they are mostly women, they are the biggest ghetto in the occupational directory. A secretary has to work at it if she wants to move into another job.

Alice Gore King, author of *Help Wanted: Female,* who has been counseling women for many years, urges women to distinguish between the "foot-in-the-door" kind of secretarial opening, and the career itself. She says that you should not take a secretarial job if "the employer is counting on you to remain a secretary; you have a block against typing; you can't spell; you are hopeless with paper work. Find another opening wedge instead."

In some companies the new techniques of word processing are taking the drudgery out of typing and transcription, so that secretaries are free to do more responsible work. The routine physical work has been mechanized, just as in manufacturing: machinery does most of the lifting, and most of the repetitive mechanical operations. If this concept takes hold, what secretaries now do may be divided into two parts. The specific word-processing work, requiring limited skills, will be done by both men and women on an assembly-line basis just as factories employ both male and female operators. The decision-making will be assigned to secretaries who will also be both male and female, and who will be junior managers, truly administrative assistants. This, of course, will tend to break up "marriage" of boss and secretary with its sex-role stereotypes. The movement has begun already with the increase in the proportion of secretaries who are men, and the enrollment, sometimes at employer expense, of young men in management classes at secretarial schools.

What kind of secretarial job is best for getting ahead?
    A job that is a learning experience, or can be turned into one. Being secretary to a top man is an education in itself. A newcomer to the business world will pick up a great deal of useful information when she works with those who make policy. Stacy Carter, a supersales-woman, says she would gladly be secretary to a university president in order to learn about the organization. And coincidentally, two women whom we interviewed, both equal opportunity officers, began their careers as secretaries to college presidents.
    In Chicago, Nellie Gifford, now associate editor for the

Encyclopaedia Britannica yearbook, was a secretary to the purchasing agent in a paper company. Because he was lazy, he let her do his job. She learned production, an aspect of the publishing business unfamiliar to most women, and her unusual knowledge eventually led to her present high-level job.

A secretary in a small company may have an opportunity to do substantive things on her own. Lois Weed, now assistant cashier of Chelsea National Bank in New York City, worked for years as secretary to a film maker and learned how to budget, schedule, and generally produce documentary films. Learning these skills helped her to move on to a more responsible job.

How can a secretary find out what other job she can do in the company?

One way is to ask. But first she must have some idea of what she'd like to do. Jane Kay, manager of employee relations for Detroit Edison, suggests that a secretary look around the company and ask herself, "Is there any job here that I'd like to have?" If there is, she should then find out what would qualify her for it. She might discover that it requires more education or training, such as accounting, or law, or engineering—then she should speak up about her interest to her boss and the personnel department. To show she is really serious, she can offer to get the education on her own time.

She also has to make sure that her aspirations are feasible. Hazel Kellar, CPS (Certified Professional Secretary), and past president of the National Secretaries Association, counsels, "Don't go to General Motors and tell them you want to write the great American novel when they haven't a single novelist on their payroll."

Well, how does a secretary—or any woman—get out of a low-paid ghetto job in a big organization?

Many women have told us how they broke out of limited jobs. Bobbie Devine, corporate manager of equal opportunity for women at Rockwell International, El Segundo, California, sums it up best: "See something that has to be done that is no one else's responsibility, do it, and then let the boss know you have done it."

All three steps are important. She believes that women have to make their own jobs.

Leonard Sayles, the Columbia professor, tells the story of a young woman, a musician who needed work, who took the only job available in a large organization, the sort of routine, clerical job that women get because no man wants to do it.

She was supposed to keep track of printed forms that were used by each department, and when more were needed get them reprinted in local print shops. When she looked closely at what had been done, she discovered a great many inefficiencies that were costing extra money. Several forms, requisitioned by different departments, were very similar. And frequently departments would not allow enough time for new forms to be delivered; they would run out of application blanks, for example, and would be unable to send them to new applicants.

On her own, she began to tell the departments when their form requests had to be submitted. She suggested rewriting the forms so they could be standardized, and she established a bid system with the printers who had been doing the work. Within two years, she had demonstrated her ability to coordinate and administer, and was on her way to a more responsible job.

Should a woman volunteer for extra duties?

Yes. Some women work extra hours, when top officials often need help and find it hard to get. Jacqueline Brandwynne, who now runs her own advertising agency, was working for Helena Rubinstein, and constantly making suggestions—until Madame finally suggested that she come and talk to her at home early in the morning. At those bedside conferences Ms. Brandwynne learned a great deal about the business, and demonstrated her own ability. Pat Pepin, now a real-estate executive, moonlighted while she was a receptionist at NBC—she took an after-hours job doing secretarial work for the head of a market-research firm, and eventually became field director for his company.

Suzanne Douglas didn't mind being a sort of twenty-four-hour cook, saleswoman, bookkeeper, bottlewasher, and publicity woman for the male executive who made it possible for her to move to New York.

Karlyn Barker, like many other young women in journalism, did extra stories on her own time at UPI without pay, to build her scrapbook. The samples of her writing in the scrapbook eventually convinced the *Washington Post* to hire her as a reporter.

These women did not mind staying late—or starting early—because they were doing so in order to learn, and to make contacts that would lead to better jobs.

What kind of extra work can a woman do?

In a small, growing company, she could suggest that a newsletter, or periodic report to all employees would be helpful—and nominate herself to do it. Since smart women are supposed to be able to write, and the job would not be a threat to anyone else, she would probably be allowed to do it. It would keep her knowledgeable about the company affairs, and bring her into contact with all the important executives.

In a larger company, a secretary could take a poll on some company product among her co-workers, and present the results to the marketing department; she could think up some plan of social action for the public-relations department. The extra-work technique will not work in every organization, of course, but many women have attracted favorable attention by dreaming up a promotion idea for an existing product, or a new product that the company could bring out. The woman with a new idea for the company should find the right person to whom to send it, and put it in the mail if she can't get past his secretary.

In the creative field, women are always volunteering in order to show their talents. Carol Lehti, associate director of ABC sports, says she volunteered herself into her pioneering position. Like Pam Ilott, a television producer who also worked herself up by volunteering, she "hung around" the studio, running errands, filling in in emergencies, and taking on assignments without pay.

Does a woman have to do all this extra work? Does she have to work twice as hard as a man to succeed?

The women who have done it say yes. Everyone who "makes it," male and female, has to at least think about their work after hours.

Extra work may not translate itself immediately into money. In fact Florence V. Lucas, deputy head of the New York State Division of Human Rights, advises women to recognize that they might take on extra duties for which it would be extremely difficult to get extra pay under company or Civil Service pay rules.

Actually, extra work serves a somewhat different purpose for women; it is one of the ways they learn because they are excluded from the usual male channels of training; it is one of the ways they prove that they can do responsible work that is never assigned them either because no one believes they are able to do it, or because such work is reserved for men in training for promotion.

Like many other women, Madelon Talley, the Dreyfus fund manager, felt excluded from the kind of help that men give each other. It meant that she had to work harder to learn. She believes the initiative she had to take forced her to uncover things that were new and better. She had to seek out contacts and explore new areas on her own. "The companies come in and talk to the men, seek the men out, but I have to go out after them." She also has to do a lot more reading.

Tactic: Women have to create their own learning experiences, their own arrangements.

Should she ask for recognition for whatever extra work she does?

Of course. A woman who wants to get out of a dead-end job must be noticed, she must get visibility. She should report what she has done to her boss, and any other superior who might be able to help her.

A man doesn't have to worry about the boss taking him for granted. He is presumed to "want" promotion; he is expected to move up and leave if he has no chance of advancing further in the company. But employers assume that women want to stay in "secure" routine jobs, and their extra work is accepted as normal, motherly

behavior. A woman has to make it clear that what she is
doing is preparing herself for moving up.

Should the company know that I'm interested in getting ahead?
    Absolutely. Many organizations now encourage
their employees to develop career plans. A woman in a
dead-end job could make such a plan herself, in consul-
tation with her boss, and with the personnel department
if she thinks they will be sympathetic.
    A career plan means that a woman should:
    Think of her present job in terms of the experience it
is providing. A secretary should find out what she is
doing for her boss that parallels a nonsecretarial job in
the organization.
    Look for opportunities in other departments. Janet
Bonnema, an engineering technician for the Colorado
state highway department, found out about engineering
from her work in the personnel department.
    Establish a timetable and goals. A woman should de-
cide exactly how long she is willing to stay in a "learning"
job, and then make her pitch to move on. And in the new
climate of equality for women, there's no use in pulling
punches. When John Mack Carter, the editor of the *Ladies' Home Journal*, asked Suzanne Douglas what she
wanted to be, she looked him straight in the eye and said,
"I want to be the Mary Wells of publishing." (Mary Wells
Lawrence is the smashingly successful advertising
woman who earned more than $300,000 in 1972 as head
of her own agency.) That's when he hired her as the first
woman space salesman for a national women's magazine.
    Ms. Douglas' forthright ambition and competence
would turn off a lot of male employers, but forthrightly
ambitious and competent males are threatening, too,

even though they can't be put down because of their sex. And though it is less common than among women, many men curb their ambition in order to preserve the affection of their coworkers.

When the personnel office is no help, what else can a woman do about finding a different job?

One way is to make friends in other departments. They can tell her where the jobs are opening up.

Pat Pepin moved from the discouraging and immobile job of statistical typist at the NBC news division by becoming friendly with "a nice man in a nearby office who sometimes lent me his newspaper," and who turned out to be the executive producer of the "Today Show." One day when she noticed a parade of girls going into his office, she figured he must be interviewing for a job, and went in and asked him about it. He said he was looking for a receptionist for the show and come to think of it, she would do fine.

Another way to find a different job is to volunteer for assignments that take you out of the office and put you in touch with potential employers. The rule that "inside" is for women is a big handicap, which successful women overcome by actively seeking outside contacts. In a job that gives her circulation, a woman can get to know other people who may provide leads to better jobs.

This worked for Stacy Carter. While at Clairol she met a man in a nearby department who was overworked. He was in charge of field demonstrations of the products to groups of women. She asked to be transferred to be his assistant. Less than a year later, he left, and she replaced him. On one of her field trips, when she was showing the products to airline hostesses, she made the acquaintance of a salesman for a uniform manufacturer. That friendship eventually landed her at Burlington Industries, where she became the first woman to sell fabric to uniform manufacturers.

The sales end of the business gets a woman out into the field where she meets other sales people, and the buyers that she sells to. Like reporters covering the same news events, they get to know each other, and swap industry gossip, including word of impending job openings.

One of the men in the office has been encouraging me to learn more about the business—and says he will help me get a promotion. Should I accept his help?

Yes, certainly. Men who succeed frequently latch on to a higher up who coaches, sponsors, encourages, and goes to bat for them. It's even more important for women to do so.

The value of a mentor or sponsor is both tactical and psychological; the encouraging boss runs interference for his protégé and can actually push or pull her into a better job.

But he also supports her psychologically. Lack of confidence is a major problem for women; they have been culturally brain-washed to believe that they cannot succeed, and the confidence of a mentor bolsters a woman's confidence in herself.

Sometimes a woman's first mentor is an encouraging father, and frequently she tends to reproduce that situation and attract one in a work situation. The mentor can also be another woman, someone who has made it herself, and would like to smooth the path for other women. Career counselors find that just the fact that someone is interested in her as a career person may give a wavering woman the strength she needs.

An encouraging husband is very important for a married woman, of course. One doctor we interviewed went to medical school only because her husband actively promoted the idea, gave her both psychological and financial support, and helped her rearrange their lives so she could do it.

Any woman can give herself a boost by cultivating the interest of someone who is eager to see her advancement.

Are some men more likely to promote women than others?

Yes, says Mary Joan Glynn, vice-president in charge of advertising, public relations and sales, for Bloomingdale's department store in New York City. She thinks that women on the way up have a better chance if they can work in companies headed by men who are innovators. If a man is interested in new ideas and products and is willing to try new things, he is more likely to be receptive to women. Recognizing and promoting women is a new idea.

Tactic: Get into a store, company, or organization in your community that has a reputation for coming up with new products and new ideas.

Can you get ahead on the job if you sleep with the boss?

There's no telling ahead of time. Some of the most successful women have come up through the bedroom, but it is a risky route. Sexual relationships can't really be kept secret in an organization and they may arouse resentment from coworkers that make a woman's situation untenable if anything happens to the boss who favors her. One thing is certain: a woman who sleeps with the boss *only* to get ahead is likely to find herself out of a job.

Sex in the office is like sex anywhere else: whether a woman does or does not depends on her personal standards and inclinations. And the old-fashioned advisers to the lovelorn were right about one thing: if you want to use sex to get money, better hold out for marriage.

If I could just tell someone how much I know about this company, how much I already do, and what other jobs I could fill . . .

Barbara Boyle did just that. She was training IBM salesmen, when she began to wonder why she couldn't sell computers herself. So she made a flip-chart presentation on herself, listing her strengths, and pointing out very specifically what she had done in the company on that job, and on her previous jobs. Her immediate boss was impressed, but he couldn't convince his superior at that time.

She went back to teaching salesmen, and to writing suggestions for improving the operation. A few years later, she tried the flip-card presentation again, and this time it worked. She was on her way to becoming an assistant branch manager.

She commends the tactic, especially for sales jobs. If a woman makes a good enough presentation to sell herself, it is vivid proof that she should be able to sell to customers.

How can I apply for a promotion—or a better job elsewhere—if I haven't had exactly the right experience?

Men do it all the time—by sheer "bull." An editor

we talked to, who had just been given responsibility for one whole segment of her company, said she knew nothing about it when she took the job. "It isn't brain surgery, I told my mother. What's wrong with bluffing? Most men do."

A woman has to learn the art of analyzing her past experience in terms of what the new job really requires, and describe what she has done that bears on it.

She has to define exactly what her contribution to the organization has been. Bobbie Devine, Rockwell International's equal employment officer, thinks this is particularly hard for women because they frequently are in jobs with an ambiguous title like "assistant," and they are inclined to minimize what they do for other people.

Defining what she has done is equally important when a woman is looking for a new job. Susan Hecht, who recruited personnel for high-level jobs with the city of New York tells of a woman who was interviewed for a specific job, and only talked about wanting an interesting job with a good future. She failed to tell the interviewer how the work she had done in the past had prepared her for this job.

A woman should develop the ability to analyze her own experience in terms of an employer's needs.

How much do prospective employers go on specific job experience and how much on what you know?

This depends on the kind of job. If you are being recruited by a retail store or the phone company for a training squad, they will rely on your college record, your general intelligence, and your interest in a career. If you are applying for a job as an actress, those in charge of casting will be interested in your manner as well as your previous experience. If you apply for a job as a statistical typist, your employer could go exclusively on the outcome of an office typing test.

A good rule of thumb: the more promising the job, the less weight on measurable skills or direct, recent past experience in the field.

Our company is starting a small, experimental new division, and I was offered an opportunity to help set it up. Should I take a chance, or is it too risky?

A new, small, unstructured situation is very good for women because it is apt to have ambiguous sex typing.

That's how Juliette Moran acquired the financial knowledge that started her rise to the vice-presidency of GAF. She was shunted to a small information task force that was being set up to keep track of new research. The function was new, and someone had to keep the accounts. It was the beginning of her interest in budgeting and costs, and it proved to be a direct route up the ladder.

Women also do very well in small companies, which have less rigid divisions of labor than large organizations. When there are different kinds of work to be done, and only a few people to do them, each individual gets a chance to show her ability.

Should I take a promising job at a lower salary than I expected?

It's worth it when the foot in the door leads to more. A woman should not worry about the salary in the beginning, but should be more concerned about where the job is leading. The learning and promotional opportunities are more important for women because their only chance is around the edges. Men go straight up from one job to the next one ahead. Women always have to move sideways.

Alice Gore King, the veteran job counselor, advises keeping an open mind on salary, and not paying too much attention to small pay differentials. A woman should check the classified ads to find the going rates for her work, but she should recognize that variations in salary may reflect working conditions or such variables as the kind of business, the size of the work force, the location, hours, or benefits.

I don't know whether I'm paid what I'm worth because I don't know what other people who do my work get. How can I find out?

A surprising number of salaries are on the public record. It's not hard to tell about how much anyone who belongs to a union makes if you know the job classification and years of experience, and the same goes for the millions of workers in Federal, state, and city Civil Service systems. The salaries of most government officials are on file for anyone to consult.

So many people work for big bureaucracies, such as the phone company or Sears Roebuck, that it is not hard to find out what secretaries or department heads in them are likely to get. And at the very top, of course, the salaries of the top officers of publicly held companies have to be disclosed every time they send out proxy statements for shareholder meetings. This doesn't do most women much good, however, because they rarely rise to those heights.

Salaries are top secret where I work, but I'm pretty sure I'm getting less than a man who does the same job. Is there any way to prove it?

Any woman covered by the Equal Pay Act can phone the nearest of the 350 offices of the Wage and Hour Division of the U.S. Department of Labor and report that she thinks there is a man in her company earning more for work of "substantially equal skill and responsibility." Without revealing the woman's name, the compliance officer will then review the company, demanding payroll records and job descriptions. If he or she (many of these officers are women) finds a violation, a raise with back pay can be ordered.

On July 1, 1972, the Equal Pay Act was extended to cover 15 million more workers. Before that date, it was limited to hourly workers, whose wages are generally known and often set by union contract. But now it covers executive, administrative, and professional workers—the people whose salaries are frequently kept secret. The Wage and Hour Division is the oldest and best-staffed equal opportunity agency and in most places it can give service in ninety days. Compliance officers expect a rush of business when women discover the possibilities for anonymous investigation and quick action (see chapter 11 for more information on legal action).

I don't like the idea of turning my employer in, at least before I have more to go on. Isn't there a less official way to find out?

Many women simply make a friend of the bookkeeper and find out information about salaries directly from the payroll department. With photocopying machines in every office, the espionage is easy. In these days of sisterhood, it helps that most payroll clerks are women who deal with the evidence of pay discrimination every working day.

Is there any way of finding out whether my firm pays more or less for the job I do than other firms in town?

The grapevine is a surprisingly quick and accurate source of salary information, and people who do the same kind of work are apt to share common interests, so it is usually not too difficult to meet someone outside one's company who has a similar job.

When I asked another woman how much she earned last year, I had the feeling she was horrified. Should women keep their salaries secret from other women?

Many women think so, and for rather interesting reasons. Some of the highest-paid women don't want their salaries known because the next-highest-paid woman in their company is getting paid so much less that it's embarrassing. They fear, with reason, the envy and hostility of all the women confined to the company's female ghetto. The salary gap between the highest-paid man and the next-highest-paid man is usually less, and white males are not confined to a job ghetto.

Highly paid women free-lancers or specialists have even more reason to conceal their compensation from the male administrators whose good will they need, and who may be earning less.

One television personality told Carol Kleiman, columnist for the *Chicago Tribune* that she didn't want it known that she made $100,000 for fear she would not be considered just one of the girls. Sometimes—and this is more frequent—a woman professional wants to keep her salary secret because it is so low. Another television performer at the low end of the scale, working for a non-union station, was afraid her credibility would be impaired if it were known how little she made. And a col-

lege administrator told Ms. Kleiman that she connived
with her employer to say she was getting more than she
was. He went along because her low salary embarrassed
him. She plans to use the higher figure when applying for
her next job—with his approval. Anything not to pay her
more!

*Can't women help themselves by sharing information with each
other?*

They can, and many of them do. Women active in
NOW and other organizations for sex equality clue each
other in on salary and working conditions as a matter of
feminist principle. And industry-wide women's caucuses
have been busy gathering salary information in many
communities. A good example is the salary and working
conditions survey conducted by Chicago Women in Publishing. Two hundred women in the publishing business
answered an extensive questionnaire on their jobs and
pay, and a committee of women from various publishers
collected company brochures on fringe benefits. For
more information on caucuses, see chapter 12.

*What do you do when you are offered a salary that you know is
too low for the job?*

Bargain for more, the way men do. One of our success stories refused to accept $9,000 because the man
who was moving out of the job was getting $15,000. She
did compromise at $12,000. Most women don't even try
to bargain, but they should. They should also be more
willing to dangle other offers before the nose of their
bosses to get a raise. It doesn't pay to be reticent about
the fact that you are working for money as much as for
anything else.

Is it okay to make up a job offer for yourself in order to coax your boss into giving you a raise or a promotion?

Men do it all the time, as a legitimate way of bargaining for themselves, and there's no reason why a woman can't do it also. It may work, but she must be prepared for the boss to tell her to take that other offer.

There's no place for me to go in my job and I really ought to quit, but the idea scares me. Should I go ahead and do it?

Probably. Women usually stay too long in a dead-end situation. "Women should not fear change and sometimes it becomes the only alternative," says Helene Markoff, director of the Federal Women's Program. "No one likes to leave a comfortable, familiar work environment that has become second nature to them, but if a woman seeks advancement and challenge, that's a price she may have to pay."

Joyce Teitz, author of *What's a Nice Girl Like You Doing in a Place Like This?* quit the *Washington Post* when a man called her stupid because she was doing a menial job badly. She decided she did not want to be the most skilled paste-pot filler in town, and left.

Doesn't it look bad on your employment record if you've quit a job?

Not any more. Many successful women have quit repeatedly, and sometimes for seemingly frivolous reasons. Pat Pepin, now executive director of a real-estate company, hopped, skipped, and jumped all over the employment map. She quit when she was bored with a typing job, quit when someone else was promoted ahead of her to researcher on a television show after she had been led to believe she was being groomed for the job, quit at a market-research firm when she got tired of

traveling, quit her next job when she found herself working for an old Marine sergeant who wouldn't let people
talk in the office, and was finally wooed back by the old
sergeant and promoted to her present job. In the course
of all this, she moved from Maine to Washington to
Boston to Maine to New York City.

"If you don't move, nothing will happen to you," she
says. And she adds, "Anyone who stays in a job she
doesn't like is a fool."

How can I quit without leaving enemies behind me?

Have a frank talk with your immediate superior, and
if he suggests it, with those to whom he reports about
your situation. If you make it clear that you wish different
kind of work, more responsibility, or simply more pay,
and if you give them plenty of time to replace you, there
should be no reason for ill feelings. It's better to ask—
in writing if it's a formal organization—and be denied in
straightforward terms before you start hunting for another job. Then ask if you may use your present employers as a reference. This greatly facilitates looking for
another job as well as giving your present employer time
to think it over. And then, when you get an offer from the
outside, he might be prepared to meet or to better it.

Incidentally, respecting employment etiquette marks
you as an exceptional woman and goes a long way toward
alleviating the legitimate fears many managers have
about putting women in high-level jobs.

Does a woman usually do better when she quits?

Very definitely. Secretaries can get off the secretarial
track by quitting and then applying for a different job

elsewhere. A woman who has become "indispensable"—but is low paid because she's a fixture, can often parlay her value into a larger salary in a new situation.

It's also easier for a woman to get recognition in her new role in a new organization, where she is not typed as a typist, for example. Women who get ahead intuitively avoid the people who "knew them when." A new set of colleagues is particularly important for women who started in dead-end "women's jobs."

The most spectacularly successful women we interviewed have been creative quitters. Barbara Marshall, now president of Welcome Wagon, says that a woman who is ready for promotion has to have the courage to move out of a comfortable slot. She has practiced what she preaches. Her first job was as a diet therapist in a hospital, a job held exclusively by women, which requires specialized education at a woman's own expense, and offers virtually no chance for advancement. When she left to do something else, the phone company turned her down as "overqualified." She went to secretarial school, and then to work for a small steel-fabricating company. This was her first introduction to money, the root of all freedom, and she found that she enjoyed making it. "I was like a kid in a candy shop, with all those things that you can do that I never knew about." So she took on responsibilities right and left, went to night school to study marketing, and when she felt she could learn no more at that job, she quit again.

This time she went to Johnson & Johnson, a male-dominated company, and got into the woman's end of it, public relations. From there, she went to Revlon, another tightly masculinist company, but because it sells to women, it uses women creatively in middle-management positions, and gives them freedom to travel and innovate. When she had learned as much at Revlon as she thought she could, she quit again and went to a company that would give her more financial responsibility because it was in trouble. She quit a few more times when her advice was not followed and became known as an expert in turning companies around.

Tactic: If you're stuck in a dead-end job, quit.

If you quit, does it have to be for good, or can you come back if you don't find anything you like as well?

You can, and sometimes in a much better job. Carol Lehti, who became the first woman associate sports director for a television network, had left ABC when she seemed doomed to secretarial limbo. She came back later, still as a secretary, but with the promise that she would be made a production assistant. The promise was not kept at first, but she protested, and eventually was given a comparable job—and another boost up the career ladder.

Pat Pepin did the same thing at the real-estate company she now works for and returned to a top post.

Both had proven their worth by absentia. Because women in jobs tend to get taken for granted, like mothers and wives, their contribution is not recognized until they leave a company.

I've been working for a new, young outfit that's started to go places. They're going to need another executive soon—and I think it should be me, but one of my coworkers says they will go out and hire a man. If they do, what should I do?

You might tell them that you will have to look for another job. That's what Suzanne Douglas did. After she had launched a new magazine by bringing in the largest share of advertising pages, the publisher hired a male advertising director because he believed that promoting her would upset the rest of the sales force, and that a woman's name at the top of the masthead lacked clout.

When she threatened to quit, she was promised the job of associate publisher on another new magazine. When *that* turned out to be an empty title, with less money, she did quit, and went on to do much better at the *Ladies' Home Journal.*

I've been working in the same bank all of my working life. I like what I've been doing, but I'm ten years behind the men I started with. Will I ever catch up?

Not there. The barriers faced by women prevent them from moving up as fast as men, and if they quit, hopefully for a higher title somewhere else, they can catch up a little faster.

I've got an exciting job but it's the only one of its kind in town and I'm at the top now. Is there anything I can do to earn more money?

Women who can't quit frequently find themselves working for very little pay for years and years. An associate producer of a radio talk show, who must be nameless here, won her title and on-the-air recognition after complaining that she had been doing the work of securing guests as a secretary for years. But as an associate producer she did not earn much more than she had been paid on her first job as a clerk-typist in the government. The problem is that she loves her job, there is no other radio station with a comparable show in the community where her husband is established. Like women who work part time and trade their freedom for pay, she accepts less money in exchange for the glamour.

What can I do about a woman supervisor who is not sympathetic to upward mobility in other women?

There isn't too much you can do to change her. Unfortunately, it's not just men who discriminate against women, and sometimes it is difficult to make headway against a defensive woman who has made it herself. Younger women executives are less likely to be so defensive and as more women rise to the top, such defensiveness will become a rarity. But when a woman is stuck behind a woman who won't move, she may have to do what she would have to do if she were stuck with an unsympathetic male boss—get out from under.

Do you mean that if things get rough in a job, you should quit right away?

Not at all. Sometimes it will be better for a woman to stay and compel her employer to treat her fairly than for him to succeed in getting her out.

If things are really bad, let people know it, advises a high-ranking woman in the government. Go over the boss's head if necessary. If a woman successfully rides out the storm, she may find herself in a much stronger position than if she had simply quit and gone elsewhere.

And quitting won't do any good if she herself is the problem. We were told about a young woman engineer who had been reprimanded for her casual attitude. She began to feel that she wasn't getting anywhere, and that she might be better off staying home and having a baby.

But when her boss took an interest in her development, she buckled down to her job, and went on for a master's degree.

Then there was a school counselor who found herself working nights and not liking it. She thought she should quit. But when she discussed it with the principal, she was able to work out a better schedule with him and the other counselors.

If I press for promotion I may jeopardize my good relationship with my boss. And if I quit, I may have to spend ten years working up to the same level somewhere else. What should I do?

It's hard to advise anyone to make a move that might lead to unemployment. However, there is a changing climate, and a company that would not think about promoting a woman even one year ago, might be thinking about it today, particularly since the advent of laws with teeth in them. Much depends on the quality of a woman's relationship with her employer, and the first step might be to see how he responds to a gentle hint. In the end, only the woman on the job can decide how great the risk really is and what her chances are of doing better elsewhere. And she also must assess whether there is any possibility that the company might be ready to revise its position and bring women into top management.

6

Tactics for Women at the Top

Does a woman need special tactics to get to the top in a big business or large organization?

Big bureaucracies, especially those run by impersonal rules, can be good for women, just as they can be good for blacks and other minorities, because promotion has to be rationalized, and there's room to get around a sticky personal situation.

However, the stereotyped role of women in the bureaucracies, particularly in the older corporations, has been very well-defined. A few years ago, an official of General Motors told me, "Women do very well at General Motors. Some of our executive secretaries are paid more than $10,000 a year."

Women in these organizations have very special problems. A man can start on the training squad and make his way by well-marked career steps to the peak of his capabilities; a woman has to do it differently.

When a woman has become a supervisor, what can she do to secure further advancement?

What every woman has to do—make herself visible. The location of her office can be important, for example. If she can choose, she should try to sit close to her boss rather than to the people she supervises.

It also helps to get informal acceptance from people on her own level, and those above her. She can take the initiative in arranging casual lunch dates. And if she has a report to make, she can deliver it personally and volunteer to take it further up—beyond her immediate superior.

Do you have to supervise other people in order to make good pay?

There's a growing awareness that highly trained professionals and specialists should be paid for what they contribute themselves, rather than on the basis of their responsibility for other people's work. In some school systems, a master teacher may make as much money as the school principal, and the concept is taking hold in other fields as well. An exceptionally qualified professional, whose skills are in great demand, can bargain for more money. If a woman is at the top of the scale for the work she does, and hesitates to switch from being a researcher to an executive, or a technician to an administrator, she could discuss the dilemma with the authorities in her shop. If they object that they cannot pay her more without upsetting existing salary relationships, she has a graceful opportunity to warn them that she will be looking elsewhere.

How can a woman who is a specialist get consideration for promotion to management?

It's helpful if she creates opportunities to represent her organization outside the company to compensate for the fact that most women are kept on inside jobs, away from contacts. She could visit influential people in the community while gathering information or making a report, for example, since reporting on a situation is sex-typed as a woman's job anyway.

Another way is to write an article for a trade paper about something the company has done. Her talent as a writer isn't as important as what she has to say.

When Jane Kay was administrator of office employment at Detroit's Con Edison, she wrote frequently on the personnel problems of women in business and industry for professional journals. Her own company was undoubtedly pleased with the exposure, and at the same time, she gained visibility for herself.

Ms. Kay has also been active in professional organizations. She has been president of the International Association of Personnel Women, and is now president of the Detroit Women's Economic Club. Club work is especially valuable to women as an avenue for outside contacts.

Should a specialist who wants to get into general management work take courses in management?

If it is a good course or school, it certainly helps. Like many women, Loretta Cowden, an administrator with the Department of Agriculture, started out in education. She was a home economist. After she reached supervisory rank in a state position, she thought she needed to learn how to help others become motivated and better organized, so she took a course in public administration at Harvard.

Other women in the Federal Civil Service complain that they do not have equal access with men to the educational assistance offered to government employees. In private industry, women often take courses at their own expense, while the men taking courses are sponsored by their employers. Any woman who would like to take such a course should discuss it with her employer, and find out if there is any chance that the company would pay her tuition.

What about management-training courses just for women—are they worthwhile?

Some management people feel that companies should simply send their women to the regular training courses to which they send their male executives. There's a suspicion that some of the training programs created just for women are "quick-buck" enterprises exploiting the need of the employers to show some compliance with equal opportunity laws.

However, many women do need some kind of specialized training for management, if only to overcome the lack of confidence inbred by the assumption that they won't succeed.

Special courses can help women define their own employment goals, and give them training in skills such as public speaking. And until all women catch up, some of them will need instruction in the folklore and language of management and the business world.

How can you tell the good from the bad in management training courses?

Any course sponsored by a well-known school undoubtedly deserves consideration.

A woman who has already taken such a course is the best recommendation—and any reputable school will provide the names of some of its former students. In large companies, the personnel department, the equal opportunity officer, or the highest-paid woman, may have specific knowledge about certain courses.

Women who are specialists in women's employment give such courses, and have much to offer from their own experience. The resource section of this book provides information on where to begin to look for management training courses.

Can you always get a promotion or raise if you get extra training?

Not many employers will actually promise a raise in pay or a promotion as a result of extra training when a woman gets it on her own. However, she can determine whether a specific course in her field will actually advance her by asking whether her employer will reimburse her tuition after she successfully completes the work. Most big companies have tuition-reimbursement plans, and so does the Federal government.

Many people are beginning to question the value of classroom work for advancement on the job. Even the value of graduate work for teachers is being questioned, though it has long been a standard feature of teachers' contracts to provide for a stated increase in salary upon completion of a certain number of credits.

I didn't get really moving in my company until after the age of 50, and now the company has adopted a policy of early retirement. Is there anything I can do to keep my age from counting against me?

Statistically, women achieve occupationally at a later age than men, in part because they take their jobs more seriously after childbearing is over, and frequently because they are stuck in dead-end ghetto jobs for so long. Earlier retirement for women than men is irrational because women live longer and remain in good health longer than men. Their absenteeism record is also better. And, a British personnel authority, Michael P. Fogarty, suggests that older women "are climbing faster and meeting more new challenges and stronger stimulation from new and more difficult jobs than would normally be expected in the case of a man with a continuous career." They "retain and develop their abilities more effectively than men."

A tactful hint to the people who are making promotion decisions might make them reconsider their policy. Flexible career patterns are increasing for both sexes, and some men actually start new careers after retirement.

What do I call other executives on my level with whom I have frequent meetings and what about the ones above me?

A woman should take her cues from what the men on her level do. If they call each other by their first names, so should she, and ask that they do the same. If they address the president more formally, so should she.

What do I do when I am not invited to a meeting that my job entitles me to attend?

When this happened to one woman, she simply let it be known that she wanted to go to the meeting, and made herself "invaluable and indispensable" when she got there. "Appeal to the guy who has to get the job done" she advises.

Do executive "stag" parties cut women out of information they need on the job?

Sometimes they do, and if a woman protests too much, the party may be canceled, and she will be blamed. In politics, women are routinely excluded from the informal camaraderie. One woman in city government reports that it took her two years to be included in the after-hours meeting of the men who served on the city council with her.

She was included in the council's Christmas party, and was assured that "stag" didn't mean her. It meant no spouses. Finally, one year, the Mayor decided that because she was included in the Christmas party, the wives of the men on the council should be included too.

This ruined the party. The councilmen needed time together, to get to know each other not as men, but as council members, she explains. The wives made the occasion purely social.

What can you do to avoid feeling uncomfortable when you are the only woman?

One government administrator says that she handles it better when she doesn't think about it. She recalls going to a dinner where she was the only woman. The

only black man said to her, "You and I are the minority."
She was not conscious of it until he spoke.

*How can the only woman in a group of men make them feel at
ease?*

A number of women in top management make a
point of keeping informed on sports so that they can
enter naturally into the small talk of the men when they
go off to lunch.

One woman pioneer surprised the company men with
whom she went to her first business convention not only
by joining their evening poker game, but by walking off
with all the money as well. "They were so worried I
would lose that my boss told me to put my losses on the
expense account," she recalls. "One of the turning
points of my career was the moment when, after playing
an extra round to give everyone a chance to win their
money back, I asked my boss whether I ought to voucher
my winnings! If the company stood ready to pay what I
lost, I ought to give the company what I won. Everyone
roared with laughter, and after that, things were easier
for me."

*What should you do if you are traveling with a colleague and both
are on expense accounts? Should you let the man pick up the check
in a restaurant and divide up the amount afterward or should you
ask for separate checks?*

A woman has to adapt herself to the circumstances.
Age can be a factor. Older men may be embarrassed at
having separate checks. Younger men don't mind separate checks or letting a woman pay the whole thing if that
makes sense for the occasion.

Is it true that women executives have more trouble getting credit cards than males with the same title and pay?

Yes, but feminist protests have the major credit-card companies making special pitches for women's business. The major discrimination, of course, has been that few women are in the salary brackets required for credit cards. However, in the hearings before the National Commission on Consumer Finance, there was evidence that a woman attorney, earning $20,000 a year, was denied a card while a male at the same salary was given one. And even though a married woman was earning more than her husband, the credit company preferred to issue the card to the husband.

Through the National Association of Female Executives, women with good jobs can get group insurance rates, car rental discounts, and membership in TWA's Ambassador Club, Pan Am's Clipper Club, and United Air Lines' Red Carpet Service, which have given male executives special privileges in airports and on airplanes.

Retailers, banks, loan associations, and credit-card companies have begun to recognize the absurdity of restricting a woman's consumer credit simply because she is married. In 1972 Gilchrist's department store in Boston offered a "Ms. card" obtainable without reference to marital status.

I've just discovered that several of the men who report to me are making more money than I am. Is there anything I can do about it?

This comes about because women are frequently "put in charge" of men in name only. Instead of exercising the usual functions of salary administration and assignment, they are expected merely to coordinate the activities of men who are encouraged to regard themselves as independent operators.

When it happens, the men conspire to conceal it. A woman's male superior may have a private word with her male "subordinate": "We've made Betty the head of the department because she's so good at the details the job takes. You are more productive, and worth more to us out in the field where you enjoy being."

When a woman is in such a bind, her authority is undermined before she starts, and the "promotion" is not really contributing to her future career. She should point out to her superior that this difficult situation is bad for morale, not only in her own department, but in the entire organization. If she succeeds a man in the job, and is being paid less than he, she can point out that it is illegal.

The boss who gets less than the men under her is likely to appear in any field that has a large number of women supervising the work of specialized professionals who have flexible pay scales—as in publishing and communications.

Most women complain because they are not paid enough. My problem may sound silly, but I have the feeling that I received a large raise last year instead of the corporate title I would have received if I were a man. Is that possible?

Yes. More money without recognition is a ploy to keep a woman from going further up the career ladder. We were told of this tactic in one company that is notoriously opposed to women in top management. When one of their best women employees quit repeatedly, they lured her back each time with a few thousand extra dollars in salary—but no extra status.

Other top women who are well paid, nevertheless find themselves below men in the corporate hierarchy. They may get the money, but a man gets the presidency.

Doesn't the opposite also happen? Can't a woman be offered a fancy title with too little money, and no operating responsibility?

Yes. A woman in a position to get such an empty token job is usually quite expert at detecting whether it's better for the company than it is for her. One financial reporter was asked to be director of public relations in a major corporation at $25,000 a year, and was told that it was a stepping-stone to putting her on the board of directors. She declined because she feared that she would not have anywhere near as much influence in a public-relations job as she did as a reporter, and because she was more interested in a future in journalism than in corporate status. She also pointed out that if she was to go on the board, her salary would have to be disclosed and that since it would be embarrassingly small, the revelation might create an unfavorable image about the company's policies toward women. The company countered by raising the proposed salary by $5,000, but even at $30,000 she would have been dramatically underpaid compared with other members of the board.

There's an executive job open in my company that I'd like to have, but it has never been held by a woman and I'm wondering what they'll say if I ask for it.

Increasingly, young women are walking in the door, asking for the top job, and getting it. That's what Lin Bolen did when she learned late in 1972 that the job of director of daytime programs at NBC would soon be available. With that promotion, she became the highest-ranking woman in any network management and, of course, the first woman in the job.

A woman who knows of an opening in her own company should point out the advantage she has in knowing the organization and its policies. If she makes a strong enough case for herself, she just might get the job.

When a company is actively looking for a woman, there is a tendency to recruit outside. It's easy to overlook talent in the shop because of the stereotype of women as nonpromotable.

How can you turn down a well-paying job that you know has no future, without insulting the people with whom you are still going to have to do business?

One woman did it with consummate tact, and it's a shining example of how to decline an invitation to the "gold-plated" job ghetto without losing friends or creating powerful enemies. She was asked to be head of publications for a leading company in her field, but she knew that the job would not put her on the road to top management, which was her goal. She said, "If I take this job, I will want to structure it so I won't be indispensable. If a truck runs over me, I want someone behind me who can take over." She was saying that she did not intend to remain in the spot forever, and would only take the job if it could be a springboard to what she wanted. And, of course, that was exactly what the company could not offer. They wanted her because they thought a woman would stay on the job. Women in "good" jobs have sensed the value put on their stability, and they have cooperated in becoming indispensable—and often backing themselves into a dead end.

I'm going to be interviewed for a top management job that has never been held by a woman. Is there anything special that I can do to prepare for the interview?

Women are scrutinized twice as sharply for high-level jobs as men, and since they have had less experience with the etiquette of the situation, they need to be particularly well prepared. Every career-minded woman should read some of the literature on how to write a résumé, how to be interviewed. She should read the books addressed to men, and particularly to executives. A selection of such books is listed in the resource section of this book.

Above all, she should do her homework for the interview. The advice comes from Barbara Boyle, a specialist in the employment of women, and Lester Korn, an executive recruiter. They suggest reading any newspaper and magazine articles about the company you can find at the library, getting the material put out by the company's public-relations department, and studying the company's annual report. Interviewers are particularly impressed with women who know financial problems of the company, because lack of this kind of information is one of the stereotypes about women that keeps them out of high-level positions.

Mr. Korn knows of one woman who blew a chance at an important job because when she was asked "Why do you want to work for us?" she said, "Because you are the third largest company in your field in the state of Illinois"—and it was the *second* largest.

In reply to the question, "Tell me a little bit about yourself," she should resist the temptation to talk about how committed she is to a career. If those doing the interviewing didn't know she was a career woman, they wouldn't be spending their time talking to her in the first place.

The answer should be that the interviewer can see by her dossier what her experience has been. She should then make the specific points about her experience that are particularly relevant to *this* company's operations and needs. Mr. Korn adds that most women executives are too reluctant to discuss in detail their own contributions, and their assessments of their own capabilities.

She should anticipate the question "Tell me about your weaknesses," and she should not make the mistake of answering, "Oh, I have so many I can't begin to tell you." A woman should pick out a weakness before she goes to the interview, make it a real one, and then be able to say, "I don't think that would be a handicap on this job" or "I think I will have to bone up on . . ." if there is a subject or procedure she thinks she doesn't know.

And after a woman has been talking for a few minutes, she should stop and say, "Is there anything specific about my experience that you want to know?" This gives her an opportunity to get the interviewer's reaction, and follow what is going on in his or her mind.

The job-seeker should also be prepared to ask questions about the company and, if necessary, its attitude toward women.

If she thinks the interviewer has any real doubts about wanting a woman in the job, a surefire question to bring it out is, "What kind of person are you looking for?" No matter what he says, he is sure to drop some valuable information. And sometimes, if he is able to recognize his prejudice against women, that's half the battle.

Finally, a woman should say "Good-bye" briefly and gracefully, and once she has left, should not come back to say, "There's something I forgot to tell you." If it is really important, she could write a note, but Mr. Korn advises against the social "Thank you for the interview" letter that women usually compose. Men at high levels don't do it, and a woman who wants to be accepted at the top should not betray her ignorance of the etiquette business leaders use in their relations with each other.

I know that men who get top jobs in corporations are often found by executive recruiters. Do they also hunt for women for these jobs?

When they do recruit women, it's almost always in order to help a company implement an affirmative action program requiring more women at the higher levels. Still, this is an improvement over the 1960s when head-hunters were literally afraid to suggest women even when they were obviously the best qualified candidates on the scene. One woman who ran a successful employment agency went into the executive recruiting business, but was careful to segregate the two activities, and to make it clear that she did not want to see women applicants. More frank than the men in the business, she explained that she would lose face with her clients if she tried to sell them on women candidates. Feminist organizations that try to sell women to major corporations have had rough going and several have failed for lack of business.

This doesn't mean, however, that a woman should not make herself known to executive recruiters active in her field or geographical area. Elizabeth Weld, director of Fordyce Andrews & Haskell, is one recruiter who welcomes the applications of qualified women. (See the resource section under Management Services).

I've heard businessmen say they would appoint more women to high-level posts if they could find them. Is this a real problem, or is it a made-up excuse?

It is a real problem. So many able women do the job without the title that they escape the attention of executive recruiters or competing organizations who would normally seek them out. Executive-search firms so seldom recommend or even look for women candidates that AT&T and other big companies have had to set up special searches for them. Martha Clampitt McKay, a corporate-community-relations specialist, was retained to recommend women for the board of AT&T because of her acquaintance with large numbers of professional women.

Women's organizations are attempting to remedy the lack of women in high-level positions by setting up rosters of qualified women. Some of the organizations that maintain such rosters or talent banks are listed in the resource section of this book.

7

Rebutting the Myths

What can a woman say to an employer who is reluctant to promote women because they might quit to have children. And what do I say when I am asked whether—or when—I intend to have children?

Theoretically—and perhaps now even legally—an employer has no more "right" to know a woman's maternity plans or how a woman's children are being cared for while she works than he has to know about the child-care arrangements of fathers who apply. Practically, however, a mother can greatly improve her chances of being hired for a responsible job by bringing the subject up herself. One young married woman told her employer that she couldn't possibly have a baby for a few years because she and her husband had just bought an expensive condominium.

Each woman has to decide for herself what job risks

she is willing to take for the principle of sex equality. A woman who believes that her personal plans should be none of her employer's business, could answer by indicating how long she would expect to stay in the job, or with the organization. She could point out that no one usually expects a man to make a permanent commitment to any job beyond a few years.

Barbara Boyle, now consulting with management on the employment of women, advises that anything a woman says that takes the uncertainty out of her availability is to the good. A reassuring bulletin is that the woman and her husband have agreed that she will be a better wife and mother if she works than if she stays at home. If she is not married, however, she should not make a point of saying that she is against marriage. Many men fear hiring a "woman's lib" type. A woman should not use a job interview as a platform for her feminist convictions.

If a woman is already pregnant, it becomes an ethical issue, and if she wants to come back on the job, she should certainly be frank about it. Most employers will carry a worker laid up from a skiing accident—and many professional women don't take more than six weeks for a baby.

Our head office is reluctant to promote women because they are afraid we will not be able to relocate if they should want to transfer us. How can a woman counteract that?

By being honest about her own personal situation. If she is sure that she would not be able to move, she might point out that many men object to transfers because their wives do not want to move. If she is free, she should say so. If she and her husband have reached an agreement about travel, she should make that clear as well. There are many possible solutions.

Career wives in increasing numbers simply pick up and go, splitting up the family for a time at least, rather than turn down a tempting offer. One such is Ruth Weiner, chairman of the department of chemistry at Florida International University. Her husband is also a scientist, a professor at the University of Colorado. Their four daughters, ranging in age from eight to fourteen, are divided between them. They get together only during school vacations, and in the summer. It's not an ideal set-up but Dr. Weiner said the job opportunity was too important to turn down.

Bonnie and Robert Wheeler worked out the mobility problem by jet commutation. From Cleveland, where he teaches, she flies every Monday morning to New York City to teach three days at Columbia University. The airlines and the New York landlord get her entire salary, but to her, the job satisfaction is worth it.

Vance Packard, who studied mobility in *A Nation of Strangers,* reports that he has come across an increasing number of couples in which the man follows the woman to her new job. In some cases, the man has the "portable" career. Just as women used to be advised that a teacher or a nurse or a secretary could find work "anywhere," Vance Packard found husbands who were policemen or mechanics, and could work wherever their wives were sent.

However, one management consultant says that a woman should not say blankly, "If I have to move, my husband will quit his job and follow me." Many men are too conservative to accept this idea with equanimity, and would worry that she is a dominating and hence undesirable female employee. It is simpler, and less threatening, to say that her personal situation leaves her free to travel.

Gladys Rogers, special assistant for women's affairs to the Deputy Under Secretary of State, is married to a man whose work, like hers, takes him all over the world. "We might have had a far less positive relationship today if either of us had held the other back," she says. They've been separated for several years at a time when their assignments diverged, meeting for holidays halfway between.

A newer and more exciting solution is hiring couples. The change has been particularly startling in universities where antinepotism rules used to bar the employment of a husband and wife in the same department. The rules meant that academic wives frequently had to get jobs in neighboring colleges that were less desirable, and the wives were the ones who had to do all the tough commuting.

Schools in isolated locations sometimes had trouble recruiting, however, because there were so many dual-career academic families, and the husband would not move to an area where his wife could not work. The obvious solution was to recruit couples. The same solution could be used to attract outstanding scholars—they would be more willing to move if their spouses were hired as well. The University of California at Los Angeles hired both Joanne Simpson, a meteorologist, and her husband, a geophysicist, simultaneously. After Maria Mayer won the 1963 Nobel Prize for Physics, the University of California at La Jolla lured her and her husband from the University of Chicago, where he had been a full professor, and she had been allowed to work in his laboratory *without* pay.

The wife's unpaid services were always taken for granted in the Foreign Service, which stated officially that husbands and wives should participate as a team in "representational activities of a post." When wives wanted to work abroad, as they do at home, the department permitted them to do so on a temporary basis, their service ending when their husbands were transferred.

But the Foreign Service has had to change the rules, if only to continue its tradition of being "representative of American society" abroad. It has had to give women the choice of staying at home, working in a supplementary job, being the primary breadwinner, or, more difficult, maintaining a Foreign Service career on an equal basis with the career of a husband who would most likely also be in the Foreign Service.

Until recently, not many diplomatic couples could be accommodated in the life-style of famous diplomatic couples like Carol and Ellsworth Bunker, but the logistics are now being worked out. (While Ellsworth Bunker was ambassador to Vietnam, Carol Bunker pursued a diplomatic career of her own, which included a stint as ambassador to Nepal.) As a starter, Foreign Service women are no longer questioned about their intention to marry when they apply, they are considered for overseas assignments even if they have dependents and, under a new arrangement, an effort is being made to assign husbands and wives to the same post.

Eileen Robb, a Foreign Service secretary in the personnel section, married to a Foreign Service officer two ranks ahead of her in the Commerce Department, established the right of a wife to fringe benefits when she was appointed to the same location as her husband.

"I fought for three years to get paid for home leave between Athens and Dahomey," she says about the time she worked as an employee at her husband's posts. She points out that the new system saves money. The wife would have to be transported anyway, and if she works, the government saves. "Before, especially in hardship posts, they ran the risk of three unhappy people—a husband working, a wife miserable because she had nothing to do, and an unmarried secretary. Now they can have two happy people—the Foreign Service officer, with his wife as secretary, working as a team."

An increasing number of employing institutions are giving thought to ways in which they can accommodate dual careers, prodded by the husbands and wives who want both members of the family to have well-paying and satisfying jobs.

Husbands and wives who received their graduate degrees in business administration together were beginning to job hunt together so they could be placed as a team with big companies.

As the military draft neared its end, nineteen-year-old Judy Bailey volunteered for the Army when her husband got his draft notice, in the hope that after their basic training, for which they had been sent to different camps, they might be assigned to the same post. In view of the advent of a volunteer army, they had a fighting chance.

I know that women can do as good a job as men, but how can I convince my boss?

Don't try to convince him in one grand confrontation. Don't give him generalities. Wait until he comes up with one of the myths about women and feed him the specific evidence that explodes it. One piece at a time. Let him save face. Offer him light, not heat, and give him a chance to see the light on his own.

Okay, then, pass the ammunition. What do I say when my boss says that women don't need money?

Tell him—as politely as you can—that the reasons why anybody works is nobody else's business. Actually, of course, the grim truth is that most women work to support themselves and others. More than a fifth of the 33 million working women are single, another 20 percent are widowed, divorced, or separated, and 15 percent more have husbands who earn less than $5,000 a year.

What do I say when the boss tells me that he can't promote women because they are too emotional, and always break into tears when criticized?

Tell him that psychologists say that men are just as emotional as women. Barbara Marshall, now president and chief executive officer of Welcome Wagon International, likes to recall the male boss she once had who stood up in a rage, stamped his feet, pounded his hands on the desk, and shouted, "I will not have any more female temperament." In men, that's leadership; in women it's emotionalism.

What do I say when my boss says that women are taking jobs away from men?

Tell him that very few men can or will do the jobs now being done by women. If the 18 million working women who have husbands living at home tried to give their jobs to the unemployed men, the country would grind to a halt. There are only two or three million unemployed men, and very few of them have the office, teaching, and nursing skills that keep essential services running.

The fact is, of course, that it is wrong and illegal to restrict anyone's freedom to work on the basis of race, color, creed, national origin, or sex.

I see the virtue of exploding the myths with facts, but can't I convince my boss that women can perform by what I do as well as what I say?

Absolutely. Square as it sounds, the most important thing any woman can do to convert a male chauvinist pig is to perform on the job and let her boss know that she understands how it contributes to what he is trying to accomplish. Neither works alone. You have to be good and you have to let him know it. Good deeds cannot be made by words, neither do they speak for themselves. The success books can advise you on how to put your best foot forward and how to behave when you report to higher authority, but it all comes naturally—and what's more, gracefully—if you yourself really believe that you are good.

That sounds good, but how does it work on the job? What do you do when men colleagues slight you because you are a woman?

Don't let them get away with it. Call their attention to the put-down, with whatever grace you can muster. Joan Abrams of New Jersey, one of the few women school superintendents among the nation's 17,000, has to attend many meetings at which she is the only woman. If the men act like unruly schoolboys while she speaks, she doesn't hesitate to remind them that they wouldn't treat a man that way: "When I talk, is it recess time, or is this inattention due to the fact that I'm a woman?"

That's okay for a woman boss. But I'm only a staff coordinator with no line authority. What can I do with department heads who won't even listen to what I have to say?

Whatever else she does, a woman in this spot should never connive to put herself down by smiling sweetly and shrugging it off. If the message is irrelevant, withdraw it. If it is essential, find a way to get it heard.

A little showmanship helps cut through indifference. A woman can do a lot to command respectful attention by changing her tone of voice, speaking more slowly than usual, choosing her words carefully, making them few but telling, and above all by choosing just the right moment to speak.

If male colleagues persist in closing their ears when a woman speaks to them in person, she can try putting the message she has to deliver in a memo—preferably with carbon copies to her boss or anyone else concerned.

What do you do when a man puts you down by wondering out loud why a nice girl like you is worrying her pretty head about these dull matters?

Don't play his game. Don't crack back, even if you can be as witty as he is, because the net result of such a dialogue will only be that the whole issue is laughed out of court.

What do you do when a man makes sexist jokes about you in the office?

Don't smile or smirk. No one is under any obligation
to prove his or her sense of humor on demand—she who
laughs with the enemy loses the confrontation.

*What do you do when a man blames his mistakes on you behind
your back to the boss?*

In this sexist society, a woman can safely ignore a
backbiting woman because *she* probably doesn't have
much credibility anyway, but a male backbiter can be
dangerous. (You'd be surprised at how rapidly chivalry
melts when the chips are down.)

Find a way to get the canard refuted, and as publicly
as possible. One way of doing so is to assume that an
error has been made. This gives your enemy a chance to
deny he ever said it.

A more dramatic way is to scare the living daylights out
of him. A male backbiter is probably a coward who as-
sumes that a woman is even more timid than he is, so he
probably is not prepared for a direct confrontation. One
Wall Street woman confounded a male backbiter in her
office by demanding that he "act like a man" and own up
to what he had said. "I put on the hard-as-nails image for
him," she says. "I borrowed it from an old Bette Davis
movie and he swallowed it whole."

This can be fun. Don't hesitate to terrify a man who
really deserves it.

What about the complaint that women talk too much?

The complaint comes up with surprising frequency.
It may be that women are too self-conscious about their
career roles, or not sure of themselves, or respond to-
tally to situations that only require a partial commitment.

Frances Dias reports that when she was on the city council of Palo Alto, both city managers with whom she worked had been opposed to working with women, because a previous woman had monopolized the conversation at meetings. The remedy is simple, and it comes from working women themselves, from specialists who counsel them, and from employers who hire them: shut up.

One woman in a high-level government job makes a conscious effort to time her remarks in a meeting so that she speaks infrequently, but always to the point, and at the right moment.

If you are a woman and you are ambitious, it's held against you. If you're not ambitious, that's held against you too. Is there any way you can deal with this dilemma?

Many women make a conscious effort to soft-pedal their ambitions in order to avoid this kind of hostility. Lillian Lynch, who for many years has been the first woman in each job she has had with Illinois Bell, says that she used to reply to superiors, "I'm not interested in another move. I've got a darn good job." She feels that this approach created the proper work climate with her male counterparts. She also says, "I wanted to be accepted for myself and my job and not because I was or wasn't a woman."

Is it true that women are more biased against women than men?

It may be. A recent experiment at Connecticut College in New London demonstrated that women have doubts about the capabilities of other women until they have proven themselves by awards, public recognition, or other obvious measures of success. A group of women were asked to evaluate artists who had painted a series of abstract paintings. Each artist and his work were described in two versions that were identical, except that one had a female name, and the other a male name. One group of subjects were told that the paintings had been awarded prizes—and in this group the technical competence, and probable future success of the artists were graded equally, whether they were identified as male or female.

However, when the subjects were told that the paintings were entries in a contest and had not yet been judged, the male artists were ranked significantly higher than the female artists. According to the social psychologists who conducted the study, the results show that women recognize other women once they achieve, but not their efforts to achieve, a prejudice that obviously makes such achievement difficult.

Don't women have to contend with the idea that women on the job have to be handled with kid gloves?

It is one of the myths that women have to overcome, but meanwhile, it has become the premise of a small industry. Both men and women have exaggerated sex differences in order to profit by them. Once you accept the notion that women are sensitive, emotional, and need extra attention, then women and men need special coaching (training courses, textbooks) in how to deal with them.

This is the common practice of creating or exaggerating a problem in order to get the job of solving it.

The author of a course in "Supervising Women" is so obsessed by sex differences that he offers two courses—

one for "women supervisors only," which assures the prospect that the female supervisor "must contend with, and overcome, many obstacles in supervising her female staff that a male supervisor is seldom, if ever, concerned with. The problem seems to be that women resent women. Can the problem be solved?" With the help of this course, the blurb continues, it can.

But first, the women supervisors need a course in how different women really are. The workshop agenda for the course covers why women work, "special needs" of women (work environment, social contacts, counseling); understanding and motivating women workers; special problems with the female staff (absenteeism and tardiness, emotional troubles, relations with male employees, health and safety, domestic complications, frictions); communicating with "the females" *[sic]* which includes "what should be communicated and how" (some things *shouldn't* be told?); "reprimands without recriminations." Of the long sexist list of topics, the keystone is probably the query, under "delegating responsibility to women workers," which asks, "how much can we expect?" The woman supervisor will also be coached on dealing with prejudices against her; "what 'they' say" (overcoming the "needles"); and finally, of course, "controlling your emotions."

The parallel course, "For Men Supervisors Only," frankly rides men's doubts and worries about women, with case studies and role playing. Topics on the agenda include "is a woman's place in the home?"; a big fat section on motivating women, which includes "belonging, social activity"—on the assumption that women are working because they are bored or lonely at home—and a section on the "special interests and needs of women employees."

These courses were offered in the 1970s. And according to Patricia Haskell, formerly of the American Management Association, courses like this are springing up to take advantage of the push to enforce equal opportunity laws. They are destructive because they are based on the assumption that employers can't *expect* women workers to behave in a normal or predictable fashion.

Luckily, these assumptions do not prevail all over the working world. Many women, most women, are treated as people on the job because most people have a modicum of common sense. The manufacture of problems is profitable only to some management consultants. But the intoxication of some of these theorists with sheer mythology means that they are no help to men and women at work.

Men who supervise women, and women who want to get ahead in their work, have to go on the basis of trial and error.

I am going to have people working for me for the first time. Is there anything I can do to prevent them from resenting a woman boss?

A woman is much less likely to have trouble of this sort if she doesn't expect it. The successful women bosses we interviewed told us, rather firmly, that they had never experienced serious trouble on this score from subordinates of either sex. This checks with surveys which show that men who have actually worked for a woman are not as apt to object to the idea as those who have never worked for a woman. Of course, both men and women who start out with strong prejudices will try to avoid working for a woman, and there is evidence that the avoidance works both ways. Several of the most successful women managers we interviewed say that they make a practice of asking job applicants outright how they feel about working for a woman, and they hire only those who sound as if the sex of the boss is really immaterial.

The other way to avoid resentment of a woman boss is to practice the fashionable nonauthoritarian style of management.

"My role was really more to coordinate than to dictate," Naomi J. McAfee, manager of quality and reliability assurance for aerospace programs at the Westinghouse plant in Baltimore, says of the first batch of male engineers she supervised. "Suggestions were welcome, and any criticism was understood as constructive."

The highest-ranking woman in a nationally known chemical company thinks it's very important to level with men subordinates. "One reason men resent a woman boss is that they think she won't move up as fast as a man, and they'll be stuck behind her. I make a point of telling them that their progress isn't dependent on mine."

There is also a prevalent belief that many *women* resent working for women bosses. The tactics for dealing with such resentments—real or imagined—are the same as the tactics for dealing with potential resentment by male employees.

All the career-guide books say you should "dress like a lady" on the job. Does it really matter what you wear?

Not nearly as much as it used to. Traditional vocational advice stresses the importance of neat appearance, straight seams, hat and gloves, and a demure, "businesslike" appearance.

Clothes are less important and less standardized now, but the spirit behind the new de-emphasis is important. "I would concern myself more with the nature of bureaucracy than with questions of dress or manner," says Gladys P. Rogers, a career specialist in the State Department—and the disclaimer comes with special force from the department of the U.S. government that is supposed to be most concerned with "dress and manner."

Barbara Boyle believes in dressing "professionally," which is of course the IBM party line for men. "I don't wear pants, but I don't necessarily dress conservatively, I do wear attractive feminine suits, however, and I do care what I look like."

Another woman executive said: "Most successful women don't dress like somebody's old Aunt Sue, because that sets up the negative stereotype of an old-fashioned school teacher. It all depends on the industry. I am in a very, very conservative company, but the secretaries go around in miniskirts."

When the secretaries wear miniskirts, the executives often wear conservative knits. And vice versa. Unconsciously we all use clothes as uniforms, or status indicators.

Isn't it wrong for women to be required to wear uniforms if the men do not?

Yes. At a Los Angeles radio station, reports one former employee, the women were required to wear blazers with the station's call letters, no matter what their position. Men were not required to wear them. This woman simply did not wear hers.

Does a woman's height make any difference?

Tall women often complain about their height, and report having been painfully conscious of their excessive visibility during their teens. But a great many of the successful women interviewed both for this book and for *Born Female* were strikingly tall. And some of them admitted that their height had helped them in the same way that being tall is supposed to add to the authority of policemen: if you're tall most people have to look up to you.

Isabel Burgess, member of the National Transportation Safety Board, and a former Arizona state senator, thinks that her 5-foot,10-inch height helped her in politics. It made her stand out in a crowd, and people were more apt to remember her.

Audrey Saphar, who built a thriving public-relations service business when her husband took a job in Rochester, New York, thinks that her 6-foot height influences her clients to take her seriously.

And if being tall is a help, a short woman may have to compensate for her lack of size. Janice LaRouche, a feminist career counselor in New York City, advises petite women to be aggressive on job interviews to discourage the tendency of men to treat a little woman as if she were a child. "She ought to adopt an authoritative manner, and ask a lot of sharp questions," Ms. LaRouche advises.

When I go to a meeting everyone expects me to take notes. How does a woman get out of doing jobs that are considered "women's work"?

Mostly, she refuses as gracefully as possible.

It happens to women on every level. Women editors are bored with doing only cookbooks, women policewomen with searching female suspects, women lawyers with matrimonial cases, and women physicians with menopausal women.

When a woman executive is asked to take notes at a meeting, she might say, "I'll do it this time, but I've got as much work on my desk as everybody else. Why don't we rotate the privilege?" If she does it lightly, she'll probably get a grin of understanding in return—and she won't be asked again. The advice comes from Bonnie Weiss, an IBM systems analyst, who reports that this technique worked for her, and saved everyone from the embarrassment of a confrontation. Another woman said that if you say it in a nonhostile way, the men will not be hostile either.

Some women believe that they have to be more adamant. Frances Dias, who made a career out of her political service on the Palo Alto city council, flatly refused to take minutes. She thinks that being chosen secretary to take notes is really a handicap because it takes up all your time and attention, and then you cannot contribute your own ideas. The men had good reasons for not wishing to be committee secretary, she maintains, and she had the same reasons—so they called in a professional secretary just for that purpose.

On the same basis, New York City nurses refused to carry trays to patients and take messages for doctors—it interfered with their professional duties.

If more than an incidental chore is involved, a refusal is even more essential. Women book editors have nothing against cookbooks; they just object to the assumption that naturally they will edit them because they are women. Joyce Johnson, an editor at McGraw-Hill, refused to do cookbooks, as did Nan Talese when she became an editor at Random House. "Of course you will be doing our cookbooks," said an executive. "Certainly not," said Ms. Talese. "That's not my forte."

Cassie Mackin, White House correspondent and Nieman Fellow, refused a Hearst Washington bureau assignment to do a feature on Judy Agnew, wife of the Vice-President, because she thought it was a routine, "swabbing-the-decks" story that should have gone to the most junior member of the staff, who at the time happened to be a man. "If I can do stories that involve men, then men can do stories that involve women."

How far should I be willing to go in "working twice as hard" to prove that conventional objections to hiring a woman don't apply to me?

"The person who raises objections, wants all her demands met, is afraid a job is beneath her, will lose out because she is unwilling, not because she is unqualified," Alice Gore King wrote in 1963. What she said then is still true, but there is no point in implying that you are willing to put up with conditions that you know you won't tolerate. It's better to demur at the outset than go into a job with reservations. An employer worth working for will respect you if you set up reasonable conditions in a dignified way before he invests time and money training you.

What do you do if your work is scrutinized more closely than that of a man or if you are expected to be better than a man who is doing the same job?

Carolyn Bratt, a physical education teacher who demanded payment for coaching the girls' teams at her school because male teachers were paid for coaching

boys' teams, refused to answer questions about her credentials as a coach because the men coaches were not
questioned about *their* credentials. She was already em-
barked on a lawsuit charging the system with sex discrimination, so she had nothing to lose.

Most women, especially older ones, simply expect to
be "twice as good" as a man, which, of course, is the
reason why so many of them are overcautious and defensive. Virginia Burns, a social-work researcher, countered
doubt about her ability to balance accounts by sending
in perfect budgets and perfect detail plans. When questioned, she has brought in a specialist—something a man
would not do.

A woman who chooses this route has to walk a fine
line. She has to show that she is twice as good as the men
competing with her, without "showing them up." If she
goes too far, she can turn everyone against her. If she is
too retiring, she will be brushed aside.

Successful women play it by ear. Where performance
is judged by quantity, as in commission selling, men and
women can afford to be overtly competitive, but an eager
beaver of either sex is less apt to be welcome in top
management than a man or woman who cooperates
gracefully.

*Don't the older women, who fought so hard to get to the top, resent
the younger women, who they think have it easier?*

Their defensiveness is quite understandable. Most
of them did have to work literally twice—or maybe three
times—as hard as any man in order to get where they are.
Mildred Custin, the first woman president of Bonwit
Teller, once told a reporter that she would have "built
the whole building with my own hands if they had asked
me to."

When today's small number of female corporate executives were starting, that was the only way to get to the top. It is no longer necessary to be a superwoman in order to succeed, but some of the pioneers find it hard to change their thinking. They don't want to be lumped with less-committed women. One of them was outraged when she was told about a woman doctor who took a year off after her internship because she felt tired. Today's woman, like today's man, has a right to take a year off if she (or he) is tired, without having it charged up against her (his) scx.

If a woman is unhappy in her job situation, should she go over her boss's head to the personnel department or another supervisor?

It would be better to take it up with her own supervisor first, since the personnel department would only go to him anyway.

If she wants to complain about her boss, then she might go directly to personnel. And sometimes it can be surprisingly successful. Aileen Callender is now an equal-opportunity coordinator at the World Trade Center of the Port of New York Authority. One of her early promotions came as a direct result of her complaint to the personnel department that her supervisor was discriminating. It led to her appointment as a special service representative.

But if a woman is going to complain, she should do it the right way. Helene Markoff, director of the Federal Women's Program suggests that she simply state the facts of the case relevant to her own situation, and not hurt her chances by overkill.

Women tend to overdo it because they have less practice than men in the fine art of asserting themselves.

I know I should protest about the way I've been treated on the job, but I find it hard to do. Does it pay?

Usually it does—but asserting herself is harder for a woman than a man because women have been brought up to be "nice." They are socialized to want people to like them. But those who succeed have learned to compensate for this reticence. Dr. Jane Russell, who did an in-depth study of twelve outstanding women scientists, found that they all had the ability to keep going on their own steam even when they weren't loved and admired every minute. This is important because unlike men, women are *not* loved and admired for their work.

A number of women have told us of instances in which speaking up or arguing back seems to have improved the situation, whether the problem was a sexist supervisor, or the physical arrangement of the office. One newly successful Wall Street woman found she was assigned to the worst desk when the office was moved. Older career women have tended to pass over slights like this, but she complained, and is now glad she did. A year later, one of the men in the organization introduced her as the only woman in the department. She reminded him that there was another woman. His answer was that the other woman didn't count, because she never fought for where she sat.

Many older women have told us that they now regret that they accepted blatant put-downs. Looking back on her sixty years of political pioneering, Jeannette Rankin, the first woman in Congress, says that she would be a lot "meaner" if she had it to do over again.

"When a male friend in the profession was unable to take a job offered him, some years ago, he suggested me, but they said they needed a man, and at that time I accepted this," Virginia Burns, University of Chicago social-work researcher, says. "Today I would go after the job."

Invariably, successful women all say that if they had it to do over again, they would have been more aggressive from the beginning.

Do women who protest get in trouble?

Sometimes. One of our interviewers who works for the Federal government lists the subtle and overt reprisal tactics used against women who protest—tactics that appear whenever women are accused of "making trouble."

Transfer: one woman who asserted herself was moved to another office. Her boss shook his finger in her face and said, "I don't want you back in this office."

No work: another so-called troublemaker was ignored when work assignments were given out, giving her no opportunity to establish a performance record, to say nothing of killing her with boredom.

Too much work: so that it will be done badly. When one woman was overloaded because she was considered a troublemaker, she went "up the line" to higher authority and threatened to charge discrimination. Finally she got to a boss who ordered that the assignment be changed. "He knew that if I didn't get redress I would go somewhere else, and I would have gone straight to the Inspector General's office and asked for a complete audit of all the work processes, and then to the EEO counselor to make a formal charge of sex discrimination."

No project work: in governmentalese, this is the extra, or future, work that leads to promotion in the government.

Jane Kay, Detroit Edison's manager of employee relations, says women have to be discreet about how they approach advancing the "cause" of equal opportunity. "If they overdo it, they find that the plum assignments go to someone else, that opportunities for the nice little extras don't come their way, and that there is a pointed disinterest in supporting projects they suggest." Their ideas may be accepted on the surface, but then nothing happens. Meetings are held to which they are not invited. In effect, their own opportunities for advancement have been diminished.

You've been saying that women ought to assert themselves, but what about the advice that we ought to "fit in"?

Even the women who promote the old-fashioned notion of "fitting in" usually did not practice what they preach. One successful woman we interviewed gave the following advice to beginners:

Work hard.
Project competent but modest image.
Don't show female weaknesses.
Avoid brassy, arrogant behavior.
Be considerate and understanding but firm with subordinates (one feels certain she means *women* subordinates!).
Don't let people cater to you or patronize you.

But how many women do just what she says—and become indispensable in their low-paying, dead-end jobs?

8

Tactics for Self-Employers

I'm tired of working for other people. Can a woman make it on her own?

A lot of women have followed the advice of Jane Trahey, the advertising executive: "If they won't let you in, go out and buy the damn place." They have escaped the unofficial ceiling on their salaries by striking out on their own in a variety of ways. They start all kinds of businesses and, frequently, they do it by providing a service that they have already been doing for limited pay, from cleaning houses to free-lancing public relations work. They are merchandising their skills independently.

Florence V. Lucas, a black who is now deputy commissioner of the New York State Division of Human Rights, was motivated to become a lawyer partly because one of the ways to get around discrimination—by race or sex— is to get into a business or profession you control. "Then

you can say good-bye to the boss when you don't like it,"
she notes.

Can a woman go into a man's business?

Many do. Jayne Baker Spain, now vice-chairman of
the U.S. Civil Service Commission and a member of the
board of Litton Industries, ran her own highly successful
heavy-equipment company. Recently, women have been
profitably running plumbing, carpentry, and housepaint-
ing firms.

One of the most successful steeplejacks in the country
is a woman, Mary Ann Quinn of Los Gatos, California.
In New York City, Bernice Crabtree runs a thriving
trucking company.

How did they get into these businesses?

Frequently, as daughters or wives. Jayne Baker
Spain inherited her company from her family. She put it
up to the employees: "Shall *we* run it, or shall *I* sell it?"
They said, "Run it," and as she tells the story, "We did."
Many women such as Mary Ann Quinn, the steeplejack,
learned the business as wives and office housekeepers for
their husbands, and continued the business as widows, in
the tradition of old New England sea captains' wives.

But you don't have to inherit a man's business.
Women skilled in crafts, such as painting or carpentry,
have begun to go into business for themselves because
the firms run by men wouldn't hire them.

*Aren't clients and customers reluctant to deal with a woman in
businesses that are usually run by men?*

Sometimes. The women have different techniques

for coping with this. Some remain in the background, hiring a man to "front" for them. Bertha Chan, who owns and operates her own plumbing company, conceals her knowledge of the working end of the business when a customer insists on talking to the plumber. She has a male employee answer the phone, and if necessary, plies him with information while he's talking, so that it can be transmitted by a masculine voice.

The most successful women entrepreneurs in male fields take advantage of their sex to attract attention, to offer extra values to customers, and to solicit the trade of other women. Mary Ann Quinn can get into the newspapers anywhere she works—her picture on the top of a flagpole is free advertising. Bernice Crabtree has been on television, though she wasn't allowed to use the name of her moving company, Mother Truckers.

Many of these businesswomen seem to be in trades or crafts in which their customers may well be other women. Is this just a coincidence?

No. Women customers like women plumbers, carpenters, house painters, and movers; women at home alone are not afraid to have them around the house, and female workers are not as apt to leave a mess. Homemakers also find it easier to talk to other women about craft work, and are more receptive to a woman's suggestions about design and color.

How do women in these crafts get along with the unions?

Mostly, they don't. Bernice Crabtree, the mover, is nonunion. Her costs are lower, so she can charge lower prices. Nonunion status, of course, means that the enterprise cannot grow very large, and is cut out of big jobs.

Don't people expect women to charge less?

Yes, and most of the craftswomen deliberately charge less to get started.

Susan Bevier, of Women Painters, says that "we amazed people with our incredibly low prices." After she and her associates got the swing of it, they raised their prices.

How do women manage a crew of male workers?

All report some trouble, especially at first. The easiest solution is to choose men who are willing to work for a woman. Said one woman boss, "I just ask them point blank if they mind, and I can usually tell by the way they answer whether they do or not. If I have any doubts, I don't bother with them." Another woman consciously chooses men younger than herself.

Ms. Chan, the plumber, is one of the few who try to manage, like traditional wives, by making the employees think that they are really running the show.

At the beginning, a woman boss may have to be quite firm, withstand some heckling, and show who's in charge. As Bernice Crabtree puts it, "You have to be careful when you use the word 'boss,' especially with men. But when you have to use it, you do."

The ultimate solution—or perhaps it is a confession of failure—is to hire women. Almost all women entrepreneurs have more women on their staffs than similar enterprises run by men.

But what happens when you can't climb the flagpoles any longer, or don't want to go out on the plumbing jobs?

Feminize the job. Mary Ann Quinn earns a minimum of $50 an hour as a steeplejack, but like other women in these dramatically male jobs, she finds she can earn more money in writing and talking about herself than doing the job.

You can teach almost anything, once you've learned how to do it yourself, and most women do tend to gravitate into teaching and writing ends of the masculine jobs eventually.

In a male-dominated business, should I think about using my initials so that customers won't know I'm a woman?

The practice used to be common and even obligatory for women in some fields but there is less need for evasion all the time. Some women do just the opposite, and adopt a trade name that shows they are female. One craftswoman said she did it because she is so shy that she couldn't bear confronting a customer who had thought she was a man.

Is there any course that would help a woman who wants to start her own business?

Accounting is a good choice, suggests Carol Bird, president of Off the Bolt, Inc., a chain of fabric boutiques in California.

Numbers are the name of the business game and many women are weak on arithmetic, business and otherwise, because they have been brought up to assume that females can't do it. A good grounding in accounting can save any businesswoman from mistakes and assure her of a decent job if she ever wants to return to paid employment.

Is it profitable for professional women to practice on their own?

There are advocates for and against private practice.

One lawyer who now works for the government looks longingly at private practice as a way to escape the hostility of women office workers and male colleagues. Doctors and lawyers who prefer independent practice say it means freedom from the male chauvinism of hospitals and big law firms, as well as freedom to schedule working hours when their children are small.

"Starting one's own practice solves the problem of going at your own pace when you have young children," Beverly Pearson, a Washington lawyer in private practice says. "You can control how much work you take. You may not be making as much or having lunch with large corporate clients, but you get a wide variety of experience, including the fun of working with small, dynamic companies." The route up in the big law firms is rough on women because it requires round-the-clock work during the peak childbearing years, and then a leisurely schedule later on, when a woman's children are grown and she is capable of intensive effort.

On the other hand, the prejudices of patients against women doctors and clients against women lawyers, have made it harder for them to earn a living than it has been for men.

The pros and cons are the same for independent practitioners in other professions. The CPA who works for one of the big accounting firms may get her fair share of the big business accounts. On her own, she does the books for small firms, and income taxes for individuals. A woman doctor who takes a job on the staff of a big hospital has the advantage of being in the mainstream of medicine; practicing on her own may mean going into the demanding, and relatively unrewarding, pediatric and gynecological work.

A lot depends, of course, on a woman's own preference. Beverly Pearson turned down an offer of employment from a law firm when she got out of school not only because they frankly told her she would have to stay in the library and do research instead of going to court, but also because she wasn't interested in the big corporate cases, and sought trial work with a human interest orientation.

She hung out her shingle instead, and has come to enjoy the personal service of the sole practitioner.

Like may other women lawyers, Ms. Pearson does a lot of matrimonial work now—and there is a lot of it to be done—at a time, she points out, when automobile accident cases, on which independent practitioners used to depend, are being phased out. Like most lawyers, she resisted the divorce work at first because it was considered unsavory and unrewarding, but after being forced into it because it is the "woman's work" of law, Ms. Pearson now finds it challenging. She sees herself on a frontier of rapid social change, with new doctrines, such as the no-fault divorce, to be worked out. Nowadays, divorcing couple are more apt to arrange a contract of separation, settling the business affairs before they get the divorce, and she enjoys working out these settlements.

When a woman controls her own business, she doesn't have to stay in any particular corner unless she wants to. To balance the domestic cases, Ms. Pearson devotes more than half of her time to criminal and torts litigation, and zoning appeals.

How does an independent practitioner (doctor, lawyer, accountant, etc.) find clients, customers, patients?
She can take a cue from the women in the bureauc-

racies who become joiners. Some women go into politics, some join churches.

Beverly Pearson has gone in for civic associations and interest groups, such as an art league. Ms. Pearson did better on her own than she did through a lawyers' referral service. Like employment agencies, this referral service was sexist. It was run by a retired Army lawyer who thought women lawyers should have women clients and "nice cases" like adoptions, and if they insisted on practicing criminal law, a little "possession of pot."

Now most of her business comes from her own contacts. "Wherever you are and whatever you do, act with confidence and people will come to you when they have a legal problem," she says.

To a certain extent, any lawyer, male or female, can shape a practice by developing special competence in the field of her or his preference. No lawyer who is also a CPA and has mastered the tax labyrinth will lack clients because she is female. Real-estate law is wide open for women as more women become brokers and sales representatives for land-development companies.

I'm not a doctor or a lawyer, but a nurse—and I consider myself a professional as well. What can I do to get out from under in the male-oriented medical world?

Nurses, long limited to serving as "the physician's servant," are beginning to demand an independent role in health care. Lucille Kinlein, assistant professor at Georgetown University School of Nursing, opened her own consulting practice in May 1971. She did it to make her professional training more available to patients than is possible in the traditional nurse-patient relationship in hospitals and doctors' offices.

She has her own office, makes house calls, and bills patients for advice, services, and laboratory tests that she orders exactly the way the doctor does. She helps patients plan their diet, exercise, and rest schedules, follow medical regimens prescribed by doctors, and teaches them to understand common ailments and live with chronic conditions. She says she has had no direct complaints from the doctors of her patients even though she advises them independently.

I'm well started in a new career, but my husband has been offered a dream job—for him—in a much smaller city where there's literally nothing for me. What can I do?

If there's really nothing like you in town, maybe you are going to the right place. That's what Audrey Saphar discovered when her husband moved her away from an active job in New York City as public-information officer at Teachers College, Columbia University, a communications hub, to Rochester, New York. When she discovered that the few jobs available there for public-information specialists were woeful steps down in pay and responsibility, she decided to try free-lancing her public-relations skills out of her home.

Her first step was to look around to see who in Rochester needed what she had been doing. The first day, she called up every college within driving range and asked for the name of the president. Then she wrote a letter, describing what she had done at Columbia, and offering to do the same on a free-lance basis. It worked like a charm, largely, she thinks, because she went to the president, the man who needed better services, rather than to the public-information directors who were supplying them.

Word-of-mouth referrals soon brought her more writing and research jobs than she could handle, so she began to search for other women in her own situation to take assignments. Some surprising "finds" in Rochester included women who had written for national consumer magazines, TV scripts, and trade journals and who were competent in all phases of research and production.

The scope of Ms. Saphar's assignments broadened from education into the arts, real estate, production promotion, and speech writing. In 1970 Ed Saphar resigned his job with Xerox to join the business, and expand the services to incorporate his management-consulting skills for local firms not big enough to have management specialists. They work long hours, but Ms. Saphar earns more than she could make in any salaried job available. Her husband, in addition to his professional activities in the company, has been able to channel his expertise to a major role in urban affairs in Rochester, a community involvement that he feels is more important, in the long run, than the prestige of a big corporate-job title.

While the demand for specialists is small in a medium-sized city, the supply is limited too. For many skills and business needs, there is no labor pool at all, providing a handsome opportunity for an established professional with big-city experience.

I need money, and I really don't mind cleaning other women's houses, but is there any way I can do it with dignity?

The 1.5 million women who earn a living by working in other women's houses have the roughest deal of all. They have little legal protection. Labor and minimum-wage laws leave them out. They rarely get sick leave, paid vacations and holidays, unemployment insurance, or workmen's compensation. Two-thirds are black. Four-fifths earn less than $2,ooo a year. They receive no formal training for their work and are disadvantaged educationally. With all these handicaps, it is no wonder that many household workers are paid much less than the local market will bear.

One problem is that household work is so unrewarding that household workers direct their energy toward getting out of the field instead of upgrading it. The result is that there were more than 2 million fewer household workers in 1971 than in 1960 in spite of an increase in the number of women with families who earn enough to afford domestic help. Since this is hard on both women who need domestic help and women who have not been able to find other jobs, the obvious remedy is to assure household workers of the pay, working conditions, and respect similar work is accorded outside the home.

To get the most money for her work, a woman should find out how much it costs to put an ad in the local newspaper. This small investment will put her in touch with prospective employers so that she can pick and choose the situation that is most attractive in pay or working conditions.

The ad should state hours and days she is available, skills offered, experience, fringe benefits expected, such as lunch or carfare, and transportation arrangements. More prospective employers will answer if they can respond to a phone number. Wages can be left up to negotiation with those who answer the ad, but even if an hourly minimum is stated, some employers may be willing to go higher to get a good worker. Doctors are usually willing to pay more than homemakers to get their offices cleaned, in part at least because cleaning is a business expense, and exceptional service is worth extra pay to professional women who don't have the time to supervise a household worker closely.

A good way for a household worker to upgrade her pay is to specialize in cooking, cleaning, or child care and get training in these fields to improve her special skill. Many communities have free or low-cost courses given by local service organizations, such as the YMCA, YWCA, or the local school system. The local state-employment service and the local high school usually know about these courses.

The National Committee on Household Employment, a privately funded action organization, recommends that a household worker refuse to work at less than the minimum wage set by law, and that she should ask for higher wages for work requiring experience or training. She can find out from the local state-employment office what Social Security, unemployment, and workmen's compensation laws apply to her situation, and demand that each employer report and pay the taxes that entitle her to these protections. She can specify what work she will and will not do before undertaking a new job. An unembarrassing way to suggest these standards is to get a copy of the model code drawn up by NCHE (see the resource section at the back of this book) and present it to her prospective employer.

The best thing she can do is to join or form an organization to campaign for better wages and working conditions. The Household Technicians of America has units in many communities. A household worker who is interested in joining can find out what's available to her by writing the National Committee on Household Employment, 1625 Eye Street NW, Suite 323, Washington, D.C. 20006.

Can a household worker make a business out of her skills?

Yes. She can take a leaf from the book of Betty Hawkins, founder of Miss Clean, of Northern Westchester. She started with herself and her sister, an old car and inexpensive vacuums bought on the installment plan. She contracted with old customers for whom she had done household work to provide a cleaning service rather than work at hourly rates. She specifies what will be done, estimating each job beforehand, and is businesslike about getting additional money for additional chores that come up after the original contract. She is planning to institutionalize the service so that the friends that she now hires can win the respect that specialists deserve by adopting a uniform with the name of the service on it. Those who work with her get paid sick leave, paid holidays, and Social Security. Ms. Hawkins is learning bookkeeping and she has registered her service with the Federal government. All these moves are not only good for business, they improve her morale. They make her service a business.

If I had a little money I'd go into business for myself. How do women get the capital to strike out on their own?

The cards are stacked against them. That's why you find more women than men with comparable backgrounds running small service businesses that can be started with "sweat capital." Those who do need funding usually draw on family money, but it's a lot easier for a woman to get money from a father or husband to spend on herself than it is to go into business. Clare Boothe Luce, the widow of Henry Luce, the founder of Time, Inc., was married to two very rich men, but she once confided that the only money she could invest as she pleased was money she made from her own writing. Savings are a less likely source of capital for women because they are less likely than men to get into the salary brackets that permit substantial savings.

Beverly Pearson, a lawyer, thinks that parents ought to stake girls as well as boys to businesses of their own. And in divorces, she believes that a lump-sum final settlement, for husbands who can afford it, would enable many divorcees to get either re-education or a start in a business that could make them self-supporting and take their minds off themselves.

Small public-relations, training, or research operations—the kind of enterprise most favored by college-educated women who have talent and energy to offer—frequently get started on an advance fee from a big customer. Other service enterprises, such as beauty parlors or small "Mom and Pop" grocery stores can get liberal credit from suppliers, just as printers will sometimes hold their bills to help a struggling new publication.

Can a woman borrow from a bank?

Yes, but she has more trouble getting a loan than a man does. Loan officers believe that a woman is a less stable earner and less likely to have the business ability and dedication required to bring off a business venture. If she is single, she may always marry and change her plans. And single or married, a woman is less likely to have the kind of salary and job title that impresses bankers.

Married women suffer a number of additional disabilities arising out of the common-law doctrine that they are not free agents. While this has been extensively modified—only a few states now restrict a married woman's right to make independent contracts—it is still the basis of policies and practices, big and small, that work against her as a borrower. Even if she has independent income of her own, her collateral may be listed in her husband's name and so less available for a bank loan; her credit rating will depend on his rather than hers, even if hers is better. Banks like to get the signature of both husbands and wives on all loans to married people, but the spouse's signature is more important when the borrower is a woman.

Are banks suspicious of a woman's project?

They certainly are. Bankers are social conservatives by policy, and it is obvious that equality for women is upsetting to their rules of thumb. One woman who wanted to borrow money to develop a line of tools and a training service to encourage women to do home-repair jobs usually done by men was turned down, even though she had a good credit record at her bank. During the negotiations, she was told that the legal department would have to look the application over very carefully, because if her proposed service had any "sociological or political" aspects the bank couldn't touch it. The only "sociological or political aspect" she could think of was that her enterprise vaguely suggested Women's Liberation. This taint is the principal reason why she does not want her name mentioned here.

What can a woman do to convince a bank to lend her money for a business?

She has to do what she would do to get a "man's job" from an employer who has his doubts about the

ability of a woman to perform it. One way is to "feminize" the proposal. Carol Bird was able to finance her
chain of fabric boutiques and get acceptance by pointing
out that most sales representatives of fabric companies
are men who don't sew themselves. She adds, "Men are
so amazed to hear a woman make business sense that
when I speak at meetings, you can hear a pin drop."

Small-business loans are risky, and if there is no collateral or proven history of performance, the decision rests
on what the loan officer thinks of the applicant and her
project. He (more than any other officer in the bank, the
loan officer is likely to be a he) is more apt to concede
a woman's creative ability than the ability to manage her
own business.

"Bankers are impressed by people with an orderly
mind about money," says Pat King, formerly equal employment officer for Bankers Trust in New York City. "If
this isn't your bag, get an accountant to put together
your balance sheet for you, and coach you so you can talk
rationally about it. If you're a doctor and you don't know
accounting, but you want money to open a clinic, you'd
better learn enough to discuss the financial picture."

A woman must go out of her way to present a very
impressive financial package, including elaborate market
analyses and projected profit and loss statements. She
can get free help with all this from organizations such as
SCORE (Service Corps of Retired Executives) or the
Small Business Administration (see the resource section
at the back of this book). If the situation warrants it, a
woman can get herself bonded, thus offering evidence
that she has passed an objective character test for
honesty and regular habits.

An easy way to allay the fears of a loan officer is to take
on a financial consultant. "Rent yourself a master's de-

gree in business administration from Harvard for a few months," one woman advised. A woman might also take on a financially oriented man as a partner—a retired businessman is ideal—to show that she will be getting continuous help as problems arise. If necessary, bring the male partner along to the bank.

Finally, advises Pat King, "Try to look like a human dynamo. Even if your idea is good, the loan officer has to be sure that you have what it takes to bring it off. If it's a product, don't hesitate to demonstrate, right there in the bank."

A young woman can improve her chances by volunteering to talk about her family plans, whether the loan officer has the gall to ask about them or not. If she has small children, she should include money for their care in her statement. "If this makes you angry," says a woman who investigated the credit situation, "remember that what you want is money, and if you get mad at the loan officer, you'll blow your chances of getting it."

O.K. But supposing I don't convince the loan officer?

Try another. Loan officers have a lot of latitude, and some are more sympathetic to women than others. Shop around. The more progressive loan officers are apt to be in larger central-city branches of big banks rather than in small suburban or rural offices.

And if all banks turn me down?

There are other places to get money that should be tried. Small business investment companies will often fund a new venture in exchange for a piece of the action, and there are welfare-oriented public and private agen-

cies that will lend money to worthy borrowers who have
not been able to get funding through regular commercial channels.

The first place to go is the Small Business Administration, set up by Congress to lend money to promote small
business, especially in deprived areas and for minority
businessmen. SBA can help in several ways. It can give
financial advice, steer a woman to lenders she may not
know about, back a loan made by a commercial bank,
and, in exceptional cases, advance money directly itself.
(For more details, see the resource section at the back of
this book.) As of the end of 1972, women were not regarded as a "minority" deserving special consideration
under SBA's charter, but feminists and women borrowers were pressing for an explicit ruling that women con-
stitute a disadvantaged group in lending, and thus
qualify for preferential service from the agency.

*Are there any laws that prohibit banks from discriminating
against women in lending?*

In 1972 Representative Bella Abzug introduced bills
in Congress prohibiting discrimination in lending of
various kinds. A few cities, among them Minneapolis and
St. Paul, had such laws, and similar measures were pending in some states.

In New York there is a state law that prohibits banks
from discriminating on the basis of sex in home mort-
gages, and this provision of the law, Section 296.5(e)
applies to commercial space as well. This means that a
bank has to give a woman a loan to buy a store or a
business place on the same terms as it gives to a man.
They cannot demand proof, as banks have done, that
working wives won't jeopardize their earnings by having

a baby, unless they penalize men for potential father-
hood too.

What can you do to get a banker to change his mind?

Public opinion is running so strongly against sex
discrimination that a sharp protest, conjuring visions of
unfavorable publicity, or an appeal to a higher authority
in the bank might reverse an adverse decision.

Banks have refused to count the income of a young
wife in home-mortgage loans, on the ground that she
might become pregnant and quit. Helpful loan officers
sometimes outraged young couples by suggesting that a
hysterectomy would make it possible to count the wife's
salary.

In November 1972 Queens County Savings Bank and
Flushing Federal Savings and Loan would not count
Christine Carroll's salary as income when she and her
husband applied for a home-mortgage loan, because she
was still of childbearing age and she had not presented
proof that she was physically incapable of bearing children. As soon as the New York Civil Liberties Union filed
a complaint of sex discrimination under the New York
Human Rights Law, a Brooklyn bank, which had previously refused the Carrolls, called to report a change in
policy—the publicity undoubtedly made the difference.
Eventually, the law had its impact as well, and the
Queens County Savings Bank gave them the loan.

In 1971 a coalition of organizations representing con-
sumers, blacks, the elderly, and women attacked policies
that restrict credit for many disadvantaged groups. They
protested against the guidelines issued by the Federal
National Mortgage Association, familiarly known as
"Fannie Mae," which sets standards for home-mortgage

terms all over the country. With the help of Ralph Nader's organization and NOW, the coalition staged a big press conference that cast bank policies in an unfavorable light. On St. Valentine's Day, 1972, Fannie Mae dropped the categorical bar against counting the income of young women and left it up to "whether the circumstances reasonably indicate that the income jointly or severally will combine in a manner sufficient to liquidate the debt under terms of the mortgage." This was an improvement, but no sure defense against a sexist loan officer who views all women as potential mothers.

Is there anything a woman can do to overcome the discrimination practiced against women in credit?
According to Del Goetz, head of Advocates for Women, an economic-development corporation in San Francisco, a woman can materially improve her rating by remaining sexually neutral on credit applications. She advises that a woman start with the easiest creditors first, such as the gas or electric company, and use only initials on the application. Another good way to establish credit is to put up security such as stock, or a car, and then borrow against it, repaying promptly.

I've had a good rating in my business as a single woman. Now that I'm married, is there anything I can do to keep it?
Ms. Goetz advises a businesswoman to keep her maiden name after marriage. Most lawyers believe that every person has a constitutional right to choose the name by which he or she shall be known.

*I'm recently divorced. Is there anything special I can do to estab-
lish credit in my own name?*

If a woman established good credit prior to marriage, and/or if her husband's credit is bad, she ought to
take back her maiden name after a divorce, says Del
Goetz, even if she has children. She should be consistent,
and use the same name as long as it benefits her. And she
should use her given name on credit and job applications.

9

Blue-Collar Opportunities

I hate office work, and I'm not likely to go into business for myself. What else can I do?

There's a whole world of work outside the office. A woman can be a forester. A woman can be a milkman. Some of the highest-paid women are on the go selling real estate or insurance or mutual funds. A woman can work with her hands. She can be a linotype operator, a welder, a school-bus driver. She can work in a hospital or a school helping teachers and doctors, if she isn't a teacher or doctor herself. And as we have seen, whatever her background, she is apt to do better in pay if she goes where the men are.

I like to work with my hands. Could I make as much in a man's trade as in white-collar work?

Plumbers, carpenters, electricians, crane operators,

and other unionized craftsmen typically make more money than office workers. Some examples from the 1972–1973 *Occupational Outlook Handbook:*

Plumber: $7.01 per hour

Electrician: $6.82
Bricklayer: $6.77
Sheet-metal workers: $6.75
Stone masons: $6.73

Asbestos worker: $6.69
Elevator constructors: $6.65

Lathers: $6.44
Carpenter: $6.42

Plasterers: $6.35

Glaziers: $6.08

Crane operators: $4.70–$8.35
Paper hangers: $6.02
Cement masons: $6.02
Painters: $5.95
Auto-body repairman: $5.51
Auto mechanic: $5.16
Vending-machine routeman: $5 and up
Intercity bus drivers: $5
Over-the-road truck driver: $5 and up (helpers: $3.91)
Floor-covering installers: $4.50–$6
Local truck driver: $4.41

In some parts of the country, rates are even higher. Amy Terry, deputy regional director of the Apprenticeship Bureau in New York City, says that the minimum in her area in 1972 was $8.40 an hour for carpenters, $8.25 for electricians, and $7.20 for plumbers.

But will the trade and craft unions let a woman in?
   The equal opportunity laws apply to unions as well as employers, so they have to give qualified women a chance. Unions are not welcoming women with open

arms, but more women are making it all the time. Doris Heflin became the only woman in the 900-member Washington, D.C., local of the Printing and Pressmens Union of North America.

Ms. Heflin is an offset stripper, a job involving preparing film in the offset printing process. She was previously a bookbinder. When she had some trouble with another woman in the bindery, a friendly boss suggested she try offset stripping and arranged an apprenticeship for her through the union. It took her two years and some night courses to qualify. The work is not heavy but requires standing all day. She earns more than $50 a day when she works, and likes it.

"The big problem is hearing about a job like this," she says. "Since I've been doing it, friends have asked me how they can get in too." She tells them to try the Printing Industry of Washington, Inc., a trade association of commercial printers in the metropolitan Washington area.

The first women who were apprentices followed the old pattern of "twice as good" as male applicants. The International Union of Electrical, Radio and Machine Operators had several women apprentices in the early 1970s, including Gloria Lang, who had started a tool-and-die apprenticeship at the Packard Electric (GM) plant in Warren, Ohio. Ms. Lang scored third highest of 322 taking an aptitude test for the apprenticeship.

In 1972 there were more than 700 women apprentices enrolled in programs supervised by the Department of Labor, working and learning skills that would qualify them as machinists, air-conditioning mechanics, sheet metal workers, electronics technicians, and journeymen in an astonishing variety of trades.

I'd like to be a carpenter. How do I start?

There are many routes. The highest-paid electricians, plumbers, and carpenters are union members who learned their trades as apprentices.

The best way to get started is to get some good vocational counseling. Take a general aptitude test offered by your local school system or state-employment office. Since tests and counselors are often sex-biased, a little determination is necessary. You may have to see more than one counselor, and take more than one test.

Then write to the Bureau of Apprenticeship and Training at the U.S. Department of Labor or phone the apprenticeship-information center at the state-employment office. They will tell you where you can find out when applications to take qualifying examinations will be accepted, and when and where the exam will be administered.

Information about apprenticeships also may be posted in the the offices of the local board of education, area board of cooperative extension services, or community organizations involving minority groups.

If it's not posted, ask.

What is an apprenticeship?

An apprentice learns a skilled trade through training on the job and learns the related technical knowledge in a classroom. Apprentices earn while they learn and also receive fringe benefits such as paid vacations, paid holidays, insurance, hospitalization, and retirement-pension plans.

What's the qualifying examination like?

It measures the qualities required for the trade. For

carpentry, the applicant has to demonstrate manual dexterity and the ability to solve arithmetic problems quickly and accurately enough to read blueprints, plan proportions, and order supplies.

Does a girl get a fair shake on these tests?

Equal employment opportunity laws bar tests that discriminate against minorities. Employers have to be prepared to show that test scores really predict success on the job for which they are given, and the evidence they submit must cover all kinds of applicants and not just the white males who may have been the only ones to have taken the tests or done the work. Tests validated on whites cannot be used to exclude blacks.

Theoretically, this rule applies to women as well. The trouble is that so few women have applied for apprenticeship training that there is no solid base of comparison between test scores and success in the training and trade itself, to test the test. Some of the tests for apprenticeship are clearly aimed at men. They use examples from automobile engines and other activities common to boys but not to girls. Girls may have the aptitude being tested and do badly just because they have not been encouraged to fool around with cars.

Is there any way I can prepare for the qualifying exam?

In most big cities, organizations interested in the trades offer special cram courses lasting three to four weeks. They are given by the local AFL-CIO building-and-construction trades council, the Urban League, the Workers Defense League, and sometimes by other community agencies. The apprenticeship office of the state employment office knows when and where you should apply.

Can I take the apprenticeship aptitude tests more than once?

Yes. In many programs, applicants who fail the test or make low scores can take the test again the next time it is given. They are usually given once a year.

What do I have to pay to take the test?

It varies with the trade and place. In New York City the fees range from $10 to $15. In some places there's no fee at all, but a medical examination is usually required and the applicant has to pay for that.

Supposing I pass the qualifying exam. What happens next?

Now comes the hard part for a woman—finding an employer willing to sponsor her as an apprentice. The law forbids discrimination against women on the basis of sex, but in practice a woman applicant faces stiff competition from young men looking for apprenticeships.

The equal opportunity laws apply to apprenticeships, and officials of the Apprenticeship Bureau would like to see some legal action charging sex discrimination in apprenticeship just to alert sponsors to their responsibilities toward women.

What do employers consider in choosing an apprentice?

In addition to scores on the qualifying exam and the impression created during a personal interview, employers consider the applicant's schooling and previous work experience. Work experience is hard for women to get because employers don't like to put them in "men's jobs." To overcome this obstacle, women are advised to take a job in a related area. A woman who wants to be a carpenter might take a course in woodworking at her local high school and then get a job as a helper in a lumber yard before even trying for the qualifying exam.

What's the best way for a woman to get an employer to sponsor her apprenticeship?

She should apply personally to prospective employers and try to talk one of them into hiring her. Amy Terry, of the Apprenticeship Bureau, advises that a woman wear sensible work clothes to the interview and come prepared to demonstrate her ability. She might bring a sample of related work. Large firms employing five or more apprentices may have an affirmative action plan committing them to hire minorities. If so, a woman can point out that minorities include women. On the other hand, many small shops hire apprentices directly, with no testing, so a woman might get her start more easily in a small shop.

How long do you have to be an apprentice?

For a carpenter, the route from apprenticeship to journeyman, including any necessary classroom training, is usually of four years' duration. In other trades the time may be a little shorter, or a year longer. The normal apprenticeship for an offset stripper is usually four years, though Doris Heflin did it in two years and became a full-fledged journeyman, earning full salary and able to work anywhere in her occupation.

How much will I earn while I'm an apprentice?

Carpenters earn 50 percent of the journeyman rate, with an increase of 5 percent in each six-month period, until a rate of 85 to 90 percent is reached during the last period of apprenticeship. Similar rates prevail in all the apprentice trades.

Can apprentices transfer from a sponsor in one city to a sponsor in another?

Yes. A transfer can usually be arranged through agreement between the unions and employers involved so that if the apprentice has to move she will not lose credit for what she already has done.

Can an apprentice take a maternity leave?

That would depend on the personnel policies of the employer, and his normal internal operations. The same rules apply to apprentices as to any other employee. Amy Terry, of the Apprenticeship Bureau, claims that it is against the law for sponsors to discriminate against an apprentice who becomes pregnant. And maternity leave has to be treated the same as any other temporary disability (see chapter 11).

When a woman finishes her apprenticeship, can she take on an apprentice of her own?

There is no reason why a woman journeyman should not take on an apprentice, just as a man does when he becomes a journeyman. And if she doesn't like the idea of bossing a young man, there's nothing to prevent her from giving another woman a chance.

I'm over thirty. Am I too old to start an apprenticeship?

Most apprentices begin their training earlier, and many before they are twenty-one. But women may be able to start later just because they are women. Affirmative action programs are beginning to provide that a sponsor may admit an apprentice who is older than the maximum age for the craft in order to meet the goal of increasing the participation of disadvantaged groups (see chapter 10). The Labor Department reports women apprentices up to age 50.

Apprenticeship sounds as complicated as college. How else can I get into work with my hands?

There are other entrance routes into the trades and crafts. It is possible to take courses in a vocational school, pass a licensing test, and then work legally on nonunion jobs, which pay slightly less. In November 1972 twenty-two-year-old Diane Devennie scored highest of forty-three applicants taking the test for a plumbing license administered by the Philadelphia Department of Licenses and Inspections. Not only was she top scorer on the written test, but she also finished first on the practical application, which consisted of completing, or "wiping" a pipe joint. She and Gale Russo, the first two women in their field to be licensed there, took jobs as plumbers with the city of Philadelphia. The city job pays around $10,000 a year, less than it is possible to make as a union journeyman plumber, but far more than Diane Devennie made before her training, when she worked as an insurance file clerk, or Gale Russo earned when she sold pretzels at the railroad station.

They learned their trade at the privately financed, free Opportunities Industrialization Center in Philadelphia, one of a nationwide network of locally supported agencies that offer vocational training for the disadvantaged. Vocational education leading to licensing examinations for a variety of trades is also available as part of the public-school system of many states. Many other crafts can be learned in commercially operated private trade schools, run along the lines of schools of beauty culture and printing.

Outdoor craft jobs are now opening up for women in a variety of organizations. Affirmative action programs requiring the employment of women in all job categories have employers scrambling to recruit women as foresters, ditch diggers, and construction-machinery operators. The advantage of working for a government agency, the phone company, or the electric company is that these pay the cost of training. Applicants take aptitude tests given by the company, and if they pass are trained on the job. And under equal employment opportunity laws, of course, employers who recruit this way have to let women take the tests and have to be able to show that the tests are not being used to screen them out. A woman who isn't sure whether she will really like outdoor work could try seasonal work, such as plowing snow for a municipality, on a temporary basis.

I'm a black woman on welfare, and I'd get a job to support myself if there was anything I knew how to do. Will the government teach me a trade?

Government policy is to train people on welfare so that they can be self-supporting, and in principle, at least, mothers who are the sole support of children should be given equal opportunity with men to enroll in government training programs.

In practice, funds have been limited, administration erratic, and men have been preferred on the general theory that the problems of poor families will best be solved by helping husbands and fathers to earn a living wage. When women do get training, they have been funneled into traditional women's jobs that frequently don't pay much more than welfare. Another kind of problem arises when both men and women have been trained as teaching and hospital aides only to find that they have been eliminated by budget cuts. A logical solution would be to train some welfare mothers to work in day-care centers, but few of these centers were off the ground and operating in the early 1970s.

Can't I demand my right to training and placement in programs set up for minorities?

Black women have found it easier to get attention as blacks than as women.

A model of what can be accomplished is provided by Dourniese Hawkins, a twenty-two-year-old black woman who used the machinery of the Manpower Training and Development Program to move into a skilled craft job as a Con Edison general-utility mechanic.

Ms. Hawkins says she wasn't really trying to break new ground, she just wanted to earn a decent living working with her hands. She had scored 99 on the mechanical-aptitude test administered by the District Council of Carpenters, but in New York City blacks have as hard a time as women getting into the construction trades.

Through the government-funded MTDA she was accepted in a thirteen-week training program for gas-utility mechanics. This was unusual enough to get her into the newspapers, and the carpenters' union sent her a telegram asking her to report the next morning. When they saw the publicity, they didn't want it and said that they had denied her a job.

Ms. Hawkins excavates with a ninety-pound jackhammer (she stands 4 feet, 11 inches), goes down into the holes in her hard hat and boots, and checks for gas leaks. After less than a year on the job, she was earning $129 a week, and looking forward to $240 weekly, which was top pay for a mechanic.

The Manpower Training and Development Program was cut back by the Nixon administration, but the state employment service will know if any similar programs exist in your area.

10

Affirmative Action Programs

I know that it is now illegal to discriminate, but is anyone trying to make employers hire and promote more women for high-paying men's jobs?

Yes, affirmative action programs are now required of every government contractor or subcontractor with at least fifty employees, and contracts worth $10,000 or more—which means virtually every large company in the United States, as well as research organizations and educational institutions. These plans are intended to change existing patterns of discrimination.

What does an affirmative action plan do for women?

An affirmative action plan forces a company to examine where and how it employs women and to compare its number of female employees with the available labor pool. The usual result is to point up areas where the company is deficient, thus creating opportunities for women that would otherwise not exist.

Each plan is different, of course, but a plan at Rockwell International in El Segundo, California, is fairly typical. Bobbie Devine, corporate manager of equal opportunity for women, says that the first step is to identify qualified women who want promotion.

Every woman in the company gets a questionnaire asking whether she wishes promotion, and what areas she would like to work in. On the basis of these results, and the reports of supervisors, the affirmative action office sets up a list of candidates for different jobs who must be considered when a vacancy occurs. The affirmative action office must agree that the candidate who is finally chosen is the one best qualified for the job.

How does the government enforce the affirmative action requirements?

The Office of Federal Contract Compliance, within the Department of Labor, administers the overall program and establishes policy and standards. It delegates the actual policing duties to fifteen government agencies, which are given jurisdiction over specific industries and fields. The Department of Health, Education and Welfare, for instance, has the responsibility for policing the universities that have government contracts; the Department of the Treasury keeps track of the banking industry; the General Services Administration has been assigned to watch over the utility companies, among others.

How can I find out about my company's affirmative action plan?
    In some companies, it's easy. The manager of equal opportunity will show the plan to anyone who asks. Other companies maintain that individual employees do not have the right to see affirmative action plans, or they claim that it's impractical to hand all employees a copy because the plans are bulky and technical and deal with patterns of employment rather than individual rights. Feminist groups charge that these employers are afraid that the dissemination of the detailed plans will reveal the extent of previous discrimination, and expose the employers to legal suits for back pay.

Is there any way to make a company disclose its affirmative action program?
    Many courts and the policing agencies agree that affirmative action plans should be made public. The Department of Labor, which is one of the supervisory agencies, has ruled that any affirmative action plan in its possession (from any company it supervises) should be made public. Guidelines established by the Department of Health, Education and Welfare for institutions under its jurisdiction require "internal communication of the institution's policy in writing to all supervisory personnel" and state that "the employer should communicate to all present and prospective employees the existence of the affirmative action program, and make available such elements of the program as will enable them to know of and avail themselves of its benefits."
    Courts have generally ruled in favor of disclosure, and according to Delores Symons, assistant deputy director of contract compliance for the General Services Administration, the result has been that companies that

formerly were willing to give the government full break-downs of the sex, salary, and title of all employees by department are now holding back this information for fear the agency will disclose it.

Many companies have fought total disclosure on the ground that good relationships between the regulatory agency and the companies would be damaged if every-thing the compliance agency found out were immedi-ately transmitted to the employees.

However, Ms. Symons notes that most regulatory agencies follow the principle established by the Freedom of Information Act, that disclosure should be the rule, not the exception. This, plus court decisions, has led the agencies to a more liberal attitude about releasing infor-mation.

If I manage to find out what's in my company's affirmative action plan, how can I use the information?

Affirmative action plans are not intended to provide a course of action for individuals; they are designed primarily to prod companies to assume their respon-sibilities to women. However, a company that has a fine affirmative action plan on paper, and is not living up to it in practice, can be reported to the Office of Federal Contract Compliance. If you feel you are victimized as a woman by the policies of the company, you can join with other women employees and start the machinery that leads to a compliance review.

What is a compliance review?

A compliance review is an investigation by the polic-ing agency to determine whether the contractor "main-tains nondiscriminatory hiring and employment practices and is taking affirmative action" to rectify any inequities that exist. If the contract is for $1 million or more, the contractor must undergo a compliance review before the contract is awarded, whether or not there have been any complaints on his hiring practices.

How can I get the government to conduct a compliance review of my company?

The rules provide that any employee may file a complaint with the Office of Contract Compliance or with the government agency charged specifically with policing the particular industry. If the complaint pertains to one individual, the OFCC will turn the matter over to the Equal Employment Opportunity Commission but "class complaints" (complaints on behalf of a number of people) or information that indicates possible institutional patterns of discrimination will be handled by the OFCC. To be most effective, the action should probably be part of a full-scale charge of discrimination. (See page 205.)

Could a women's caucus or committee support a request for a compliance review?

Absolutely. Organized women's groups are in a good position to make damaging statements to compliance officers when reviews are made. That's one reason why companies are extremely cautious in dealing with women's caucuses. (For more on caucuses, see chapter 12.)

What happens if the compliance review turns up evidence of noncompliance?

If the contractor does not bring his policies into

compliance, or show evidence that he is working toward it, the government has the right to cancel or terminate the contract.

Have any contracts actually been canceled?

Contracts for a few universities have been held up, and the word is out in other organizations. The threat of cancellation has been enough reason for companies to take women seriously.

If companies are afraid of cancellation of contracts for noncompliance, then why don't we get more action?

Because enforcement officials are sometimes reluctant and always overloaded with work. First-line supervisors and middle managers resist change, and fear that their authority will be threatened, just as they did when they were required to hire and promote blacks in the 1950s and 1960s. Their employers had to set up special programs to educate and condition these managers to think and act color blind, and the employers are now buying training programs to do the same job with their middle managers on women.

Will employers have to go out hunting for top-level women to hire and promote the way they went out of their way to recruit blacks during the 1960s?

Many women are hoping that it will work out that way, and despite employers' protests to the contrary, qualified women are not hard to find. Every big organization has a few under-utilized women who can be quickly and easily promoted to top-level posts, and a number of women have profited from the new requirements.

A good example from the Federal service is Bette A. Krenzer, the electronics engineer who started as a technician and had managed to get a degree and on the professional ladder at Wright-Patterson Air Field. When President Nixon ordered an increase in the number of women at the highest Civil Service grades, she had already spent five years at Grade 13, which was the unwritten ceiling on women at her installation. She was promoted by direct intervention of the base commander.

Jane Kay, the highest-ranking woman in the Detroit Edison Company, was probably helped in her elevation to manager of employee relations for the entire company by the push to show women in positions at the top. Ms. Kay worked for the company on a part-time basis when she was in college and, after graduation, went into a program for training personnel interviewers. The sex segregation of the company's employment practices was actually an asset to her career development, just as race segregation of schools and churches had provided opportunities for black professionals. At the time she was hired, there was a special women's division in personnel. Women office workers were interviewed by women interviewers, and evaluated and promoted according to a separate female schedule.

"Because the turnover of women interviewers was greater than for men, I was able to get into more responsible staff jobs than beginning male interviewers," she recalls. Ten years later, the male and female divisions were integrated, largely because company administrators discovered considerable duplication of effort and less difference in the techniques required than formerly imagined. She was then in a good spot for a top position in the combined operation. In spite of the help that she received in the beginning from sex segregation, she has become an outspoken and informed champion of equal opportunity for women. "I've always felt that a women had to be more competent than a man to get as far as he," she says, "and now I feel an obligation to show that a woman can be successful when given the chance."

Can't the companies just say that they don't have more women in high-level jobs because they can't find them?

The absence of qualified women is no longer a defense against a charge that women are underutilized. If the company does not have, and can't find, qualified women, it must use special recruiting methods. That's one reason feminist groups are compiling talent rosters. Furthermore, companies have to consider training their female employees as a means of upgrading women into the better jobs.

Aren't some of these women in made up jobs, like "Coordinator of Women's Programs"?

Don't knock these new jobs. Equal opportunity can't be created simply by decreeing it. It takes people with nothing else to do but stand watch over employment practices. The Federal government had been ordering merit promotion for more than a generation, but blacks did not start really moving up the ladder until equal opportunity officers were stationed in Federal agencies and the offices of their civilian contractors. In most agencies, these EEO's are now concerned with women employees as well as blacks, but the double responsibility doesn't work very well even though the methods are similar. Specialists in personnel say that the quickest way to find out whether women are actually moving ahead in an organization is to see whether the table of organization has a woman who does nothing but watch out for the rights of women employees.

Maybe so, but aren't they just taking advantage of discrimination against women to create good jobs for themselves?

Not if they are really helping other women. If safeguarding equal opportunity is worthwhile work—and we believe that it is—it deserves worthwhile payment. It takes skill and it isn't easy.

Jane Kay, at Detroit Edison, has been both firm and successful in asserting that women actually are underprivileged on the job, and she has instituted reforms that have improved the lot of all Detroit Edison women.

Bobbie Devine has done the same for women at Rockwell International. She became interested in legislation as it affects personnel at a time when no one in the company was particularly interested or worried about it. She took the initiative to ask her boss if she could work in this area, and pointed out that pending laws about employment discrimination could make a great deal of difference to the company. When the laws were passed, she was in line for a more important job in the company, and Rockwell International had a head start in complying.

Hasn't equal opportunity work created jobs for black women that pay more than they would otherwise be able to get?

Yes, it has. And there are sound reasons why. Many of the first equal opportunity officers were black. It made sense not only because a black face on the administrative staff was an earnest of good faith in promoting blacks, but because the new post offered an opportunity to increase the number of blacks in good jobs. When women were added to the affirmative action order, many of these black men found it hard to sympathize with the plight of white women. The obvious link between the two oppressed "minorities" was a black woman who could sympathize with both groups and hopefully mediate between them in competition for staff and funds. And just as the first black EEO's served partly as symbols of the cause they were promoting, so black women do double service as double tokens.

Eleanor Holmes Norton did a lot to raise the morale of both blacks and women when, at the age of thirty-two, she was made commissioner of human rights for New York City at a salary of $30,000 a year.

Aileen Callendar is one of the many black women who broke out of the female job ghetto and created a professional career for herself out of equal opportunity work. She was doing community-relations work for the Port of New York Authority (PONY). She helped manage the protocol department, which greets visitors, but when she asked to go into the field, to take visitors on tours, she was turned down. (Women always have trouble getting outside jobs.) She took her complaint to the personnel department, maintaining that PONY, as a public agency, should certainly not discriminate. She was transferred within a few months, and meanwhile, had become visible. When PONY needed an equal opportunity officer to mediate between white contractors and black community leaders during the construction of the World Trade Center, Ms. Callendar was the logical person for the job.

11

The Legal Route

What is discrimination—legally?

The law requires equal treatment of men and women. If hiring or promotional preference is given to one sex, that's discrimination. If men are paid more than women for the same work, that's discrimination. If offices, or company cars, or lunch hours, or privileges of any kind are assigned on the basis of sex, that's discrimination. These discrepancies seem so natural that most employers and employees are just beginning to recognize that they are illegal. In January 1973 the government called for back payment to 15,000 employees of American Telephone and Telegraph, including 13,000 women who might have had better-paying jobs if the company did not have a long history of discrimination. The settlement recognized that a woman does not have to ask for the better job in order to suffer damages be-

cause it would never have occurred to her to apply for
a job that company policy reserves for men. AT&T
agreed to pay lump-sum damages to the women who had
just begun to move into craft jobs from which they had
previously been excluded. The employment committee
of the New York chapter of the National Organization for
Women (NOW) points out, however, that *equal* treatment of men and women is not the same as fair treatment
toward all employees. If a boss mistreats everyone, it's
not discrimination. But if he acts that way only toward
women, it is illegal. If you are not sure whether a particular action or practice is discriminatory, NOW suggests
that you ask yourself, "Would this be happening to me
if I were a white male?" If the answer is "no," you have
a basis for a complaint.

*I know I'm being discriminated against right now. Talking hasn't
helped, and I don't want to quit. Can I sue?*

Any woman who believes she is not being given a
fair shake can start the legal machinery moving on her
own behalf in a variety of ways. In addition to stirring up
a compliance review via the OFCC, there are two other
legislative vehicles for bringing a complaint: the Equal
Pay Act of 1963, amended in 1972, which pertains only
to pay and fringe benefits; and Title VII of the Civil
Rights Act of 1964, as amended by the Equal Employment Opportunity Act of 1972, which bans any form of
job discrimination based on race, color, religion, sex, or
national origin.

*I think I'm being paid less than the men in my office who do the
same work. What law covers that?*

That situation is covered by the Equal Pay Act and really is the easiest form of discrimination to fight. With a few exceptions, everyone is covered who works for salary or wages in an office or organization that employs two or more people. To find out if your employer is covered, send for the Equal Pay booklet. Write to Morag Simchak, Special Assistant to the Assistant Secretary of Labor for Employment Standards, U.S. Department of Labor, Washington, D.C. 20210.

How do I file a complaint under the Equal Pay Act?
Write or phone the nearest of the 350 local Wage and Hour offices (listed under U.S. Government, Labor Department, in the telephone book). There are no special forms to fill out—a letter or phone call is enough to start an investigation. They won't even insist upon having your name. Usually, however, a compliance officer is assigned to interview the complainant confidentially, and then visits her employer to examine the evidence without revealing her name. The compliance officer will look at all the company records, including payroll records, union agreements, and job descriptions. If evidence of pay discrimination is found, the department will seek voluntary compliance. In most cases, this is enough, but if not, the case can be taken to court by the Labor Department or by the employee herself. The enforcement of this law is usually fast and efficient. The Wage and Hour Division has a large staff of highly trained compliance officers.

Will the Equal Pay people really keep my name out of it?
Yes. The procedures under the Equal Pay Act are

very specific about protecting the complainant's identity; Labor Department investigators take every precaution to protect anonymity. When an investigator goes in, he or she looks at all company practices, not just one specific area that might tip off the employer to the name of the complainant. In addition, the Wage and Hour people routinely make spot checks on companies, so the firm has no way of knowing whether a complaint has actually been filed. Department spokesmen point out that in many years of enforcement, there has never been a breach of confidence. If the case has to go to court, however, the Labor Department may want to use your name, but the name will not be revealed without your permission (and 95 percent of all Equal Pay cases do not get to court).

Will I get back pay if the case is decided in my favor?
   Very possibly. The Department of Labor says that close to $50 million in back pay has been found owing to more than 100,000 women under the Equal Pay Act. In a case that did go to court, female nurses' aides in Roseville, California, claimed that they did the same work as male orderlies, and the Roseville Hospital was ordered to reimburse 60 women more than $27,000. Hundreds of thousands of dollars have already been paid to aggrieved employees, both because of court rulings and voluntary out-of-court settlements.

How many years of back pay could I get?
   Since the law was amended in 1972, there has been a two-year statute of limitations, though in some earlier settlements, back pay had been granted for longer periods.

What exactly does the Equal Pay Act cover?

Situations in which women are paid less than men for substantially the same work. Titles and job descriptions don't matter. The investigators look at the work done. If the work done by men and women is substantially the same, the pay must be the same, although the law does allow certain exceptions, as, for example, when one employee has years of seniority over other employees.

I work in a factory. The men who work here do exactly what the women do, but they get paid $.75 an hour more because some of them unpack crates of material at the beginning of the shift. Is that legal?

The courts have said no. The Equal Pay Act of 1963 called for equal pay to men and women for work "which requires equal skill, effort, and responsibility." At first some employees tried to justify different wage scales by assigning extra duties to the men. But in 1970 a court in New Jersey ruled that jobs did not have to be identical, only "substantially equal."

In that case, the evidence showed that both men and women were hired by the Wheaton Glass Company to inspect glass bottles, discard bad ones, and pack the good ones into cartons. The men were paid $2.35½ an hour, the women $2.14. Some of the men occasionally performed extra duties that were usually done by boys who earned $2.16 an hour.

The court found that the extra work did not justify the higher pay for the men because the boys who regularly did the work were paid less, and because most of the time the men and women did the same work. Furthermore, no attempt was made to find out if the women would or could do the extra tasks, and thus earn the extra pay. The court concluded that the wage difference was based on sex, and the Wheaton Glass Company was ordered to pay the women back wages and interest totaling more than $900,000.

I sell women's coats in a department store. We've always accepted the fact that the men who sell men's clothing make more money —and get a commission—but isn't this now illegal?
     Yes, it is a violation of the Equal Pay Act, according to a district court in Alabama. A department store in Montgomery justified different pay scales for salesmen and saleswomen by claiming that different skills are needed to sell different kinds of merchandise.
     The court rejected the store's arguments, including one that male customers are more difficult to please because they don't know what they want. On the contrary, the court felt that because a woman has "sharpened and refined tastes," *she* would be more difficult to satisfy.

But where do I go to complain about not getting hired or not getting promoted because I'm a woman?
     All forms of discrimination—subtle and not so subtle—are covered by Title VII of the Civil Rights Act of 1964, as amended by the Equal Employment Opportunity Act of 1972. The Equal Employment Opportunity Commission (EEOC) was created specifically to administer this law and handles complaints by individual women or by groups of women.

Who is covered under Title VII?
     Employees of private and public businesses, institu-

tions, and organizations. The amended law of 1972 extended coverage to employees of educational institutions who used to be exempt as well as to employees of state and local governments. Federal employees are covered under a separate Executive order. Since March 1973 the law that formerly applied to employers with twenty-five or more employees has covered employers with fifteen or more employees.

Where do I file a charge of employment discrimination because I'm a woman?

With every possible agency: The Federal Equal Employment Opportunity Commission at 1800 G Street, Washington, D.C. 20506, the state or municipal fair employment-practices agency, the local office of the U.S. Department of Labor, or the state agency administering an equal pay law, and the Office of Contract Compliance, if the employer is a Federal contractor.

The EEOC may defer to the state fair employment practices agency, but it is to a woman's advantage to have her complaints in the Federal EEOC system at the same time. Government experts and women's rights groups all advise filing simultaneously with every agency that will accept the complaint.

How do I file a charge?

An EEOC charge form can be obtained from the local EEOC office, but it is not necessary. All that is required is a written statement from the person filing the complaint, identifying the employer, and describing in general terms the action or practices that are causing her trouble. The local agency, or the National Organization for Women (NOW), can offer advice on how to word the complaint.

NOW has been very active in assisting individual women with discrimination problems. Not only does the organization have a number of informative booklets, but most chapters have trained lay counselors ready to work with individual women and guide them through the maze of agencies and laws.

If you can't find a NOW chapter in your local phone book, write to the national office, National Organization for Women, 1957 East 73rd Street, Chicago, Illinois 60649.

Is there any time limit for filing with the EEOC?

Yes, in some cases. Time limitations vary with the circumstances, so it is best to file a charge as soon as possible.

Will my complaint go right to court?

No. The charge is first investigated by the Commission itself, or by a state agency, if one exists. Then, the Commission will try to reach an agreement with the employer to rectify the procedure. If no agreement can be reached, the EEOC can bring a court action against the employer.

Don't I need documents to prove discrimination?

No, you don't have to have positive proof to get an investigation started. The equal pay and equal opportunity agencies need only your suspicion that discrimination exists. It's the government's job to get the evidence.

Agency spokesmen do say, however, that they find it helpful if you tell them as much as possible about the company's employment practices. Sometimes, a woman can strengthen her case by comparing her advancement with that of a man with comparable credentials.

What kind of remedies can I expect from the EEOC or the courts if my case is decided in my favor?

The EEOC or the courts may call for any one or several of a number of remedies, such as reinstatement, hiring, back pay, and a correction of the discriminatory practice, not only for the complainant, but for other women similarly situated.

Do I need a lawyer?

The agencies themselves say no. However, many EEOC offices have a backlog of cases, and the number of complaints is increasing all the time. If the agencies do not take timely action, a woman will need a lawyer in order to go to court. And some women have had to go to court for enforcement even though the agencies found that their complaints were justified.

Janet P. Bonnema's two-year battle to get inside a highway tunnel is a case in point. The barrier she faced was a superstition that women are bad luck in underground projects such as tunnels and mines.

It began in December 1970 when Ms. Bonnema took, and passed, the Colorado Civil Service exam that would enable her to work as an engineering technician. She was, in fact, first on the eligible list for state-wide positions with the department of highways. Almost immediately, she was offered a position on the Straight Creek

Tunnel project. The offer came in a letter addressed to Mr. Jamet P. Bonnema. When she phoned about the position a few days later, she was told that women were not allowed in tunnels, and that therefore the job was open only to men. She then filed a formal complaint—the first of several—with the Colorado Civil Rights Commission, and within two months, the job offer was renewed. This time, however, the letter specified that her assignment would be "in the office performing various office engineering-type duties."

When she reported for work, she realized that the office job had been created just for her, and that she was the only engineering technician not to be allowed into the tunnel under any circumstances.

She also learned that the tunnel was an unusual project, employing revolutionary new mining techniques that were attracting visitors from all over the world. Male foreign engineers, male journalists, and male photographers all went into the tunnel, but no females, including Ms. Bonnema and women reporters.

Her charge now was that by excluding her from the tunnel, the highway department was denying her job experience that would enable her to progress further in her career, a denial that was based solely on sex.

The matter became urgent as the tunnel neared completion, and she hired a lawyer to get fast action. But even though state and Federal agencies repeatedly found that her complaint was justified, the state highway department continued to stall. Finally, in October 1972 she asked for, and was granted, a court order requiring the highway department to admit her to the tunnel immediately. Accompanied by newspaper photographers and reporters, one of whom was another woman, Ms. Bonnema had an orientation tour of the almost-finished tunnel, a tour that she would have received on her first day of work two years earlier if she had been a man.

Is legal help available if I should want to sue on a charge of job discrimination?

Women's law groups will take cases that are particularly important because they break new ground, and set new precedents. Hundreds of charges of sex discrimination are in the courts now, and many others could be brought if the women involved could afford lawyers.

We have listed sources for women who want legal advice and help in the resource section at the back of the book, but these sources have told us that they cannot help more than a few individual women.

What if there are a number of women being treated unfairly? Do we all have to file a charge or is it enough if one of us does it?

Technically, one person can file on behalf of everyone in what is called a "class action," but there is job safety in numbers. An employer is not likely to fire everybody so it is better—and makes a stronger case—to get everyone together and file a charge with a number of names. Then, if it does become necessary to go to court, everyone can contribute toward hiring a lawyer.

What happens to the women you read about who sue on charges of sex discrimination?

The main result, if they are successful, is that they do a large amount of good for all other women. What happens to their own careers is something else again.

Many of them find that their lives are changed by the experience, frequently for the better in unexpected ways.

Carolyn Bratt was a history teacher in the Syracuse, New York, school system, when she was asked to coach the junior-high girls' basketball team, which played against other junior-high teams in the city. She agreed, and then discovered that a similar boys' basketball team was coached by a math teacher, who received $308 for the extra job, while she was paid nothing.

Ms. Bratt went through every possible grievance channel, her principal, the superintendent of schools, the Syracuse Teachers Association, to which she belonged, and the board of education. All down the line she was told that the activity was not provided for in her contract, and what she was doing was an extra-curricular activity, for which no teacher was paid, but for the man, it was intramural, and his pay came out of the sports budget. She did not think the distinction was valid.

She was also under pressure from teachers in her own school, who were afraid that the whole girls' program would be scrapped if coaching had to be paid for. The problem was that the sports budget simply did not contain enough money to pay for coaches for both boys and girls.

When she could do nothing further with the school system, she went to the New York State Division of Human Rights and filed a complaint. Three years later, the girls' program had been changed, to eliminate the need for coaches, and her case was still pending, awaiting a decision by the New York State Court of Appeals as to whether the New York State Division of Human Rights had jurisdiction. Meanwhile, the long court battle had interested her in a legal career, and she had left teaching to go to law school.

I work for the city. Are local government employees covered by Title VII?

The newest amendments do include state and local government employees, and Federal workers are covered under their own laws. A charge was recently filed against the city of Dallas, Texas, claiming that the city was not actively improving the proportion of women in administrative and blue-collar positions, that it did not allow women to do police patrol work, or fire-fighting, and that its maternity leave policy violated EEOC guidelines.

No agency or organization is immune from charges of sex discrimination. Women in the offices of the Equal Employment Opportunity Commission itself have filed charges claiming that the agency's personnel policies favor men.

Are there any reasons, based on sex, that an employer may use to refuse employment to a woman?

Yes. The EEOC has established and published guidelines to help employers and employees recognize discrimination, and they have said that sex may be used as a criterion when there is a "bona fide occupational qualification," abbreviated to BFOQ. However, both the commission and the courts have held that this condition must be interpreted very narrowly. There has to be a really compelling reason for a sexual preference, such as hiring a woman for a woman's role in a play, or a woman to model women's clothes.

I'd like to work overtime and make some extra money the way men do. My foreman says I can't because state law puts a limit on the amount of overtime a woman can work. Is he right?

No. The EEOC has concluded that many state laws that claim to protect women actually deny them equal opportunity and are superseded by new Federal laws. The courts have upheld this view.

I was turned down for a job because I'd have to work in a place where there is no separate toilet for women—and that's against a state law. Is this legal?

Probably not. Employers cannot refuse to hire women because state laws call for special conditions for them, such as minimum wages, overtime pay, rest periods, or separate physical facilities.

I can't get the job I want because the work involves lifting more weight than the state law allows for women. Can I sue for the job?

Yes. Immediately after the passage of the equal opportunity law of 1964, the courts tended to support employers who cited such state protective laws. They went along with the views of one labor arbitrator who believed that medical authorities supported the notion of restricting heavy work for women "because of the physical nature and function of their bodies." But in August 1969 new EEOC guidelines said that state laws regulating hours and weight lifting could not be used to keep women out of jobs: "The Commission has found that such laws and regulations do not take into account the capacities, preferences, and abilities of individual females and tend to discriminate rather than protect." A court in Georgia said much the same thing: "Title

VII rejects romantic paternalism as unduly Victorian, and instead vests individual women with the power to decide whether or not to take on unromantic tasks. Men have always had the right to determine whether the incremental increase in remuneration for strenuous, dangerous, obnoxious, boring or unromantic tasks is worth the candle." The court said that women should have the same right.

But don't some of these protective laws keep women from being exploited?

Men need to be protected from exploitation also. Many labor laws now extended to all workers began as special protections for women. A thirty-minute lunch break, required in some states for women, will probably be extended to men. There are practical, as well as moral, reasons for this—in a big organization it is administratively easier to treat all workers alike.

Of course, "protection" means different things to different women. One woman may regard a limit on overtime or weight lifting as protection, another woman may call the same limit a barrier that keeps her from getting a better job.

In my company, the men have always had more freedom and privileges than the women. Is this illegal?

Yes. Title VII requires equal "conditions of employment," and the EEOC has ruled against employers who allow males but not females to smoke on the job, or who issue a dress code for women while allowing the men to wear what they please. Charges have been brought against employers who deny women the use of the executive dining room provided for men of the same rank. In Atlanta, Georgia, Sandra Drew charged Liberty Mutual Insurance Company with paying her less than men who did the same work, denying her use of a company car, and not allowing her to settle claims outside the office, privileges that the men enjoyed.

I am working toward a promotion, but supervisors are required to have certain training and the company training program seems to have only men in it. Is this legal?

No. It is discriminatory if qualified women are excluded. Women are entitled to the same training opportunities as men. Denial of such opportunities is a violation of the equal opportunity laws.

Do I have a case for sex discrimination because a man with no more qualifications than mine, was promoted over me?

It would depend on the circumstances. In one case, a state agency ruled that no discrimination was involved because the man had asked for the job, and the woman had not.

Some cases are hard to prove because the employer has the right to set standards. "It is hard to judge whether three years of college and two of experience is worth more than four years of college and one of experience," says Florence V. Lucas, deputy commissioner of the New York State Division of Human Rights.

An employer may undertake, in his affirmative action program, to review all employees before promoting one, or to post job openings so that all employees may apply. Then, if he does not actually do so, he can be charged.

But failure to take these steps in the absence of an affirmative action program is not ground for suit per se. You can't ask an employer to comb through the merits of a thousand employees—he'd need a computer to decide where the hair's breadth of experience differed.

I was fired because I was out sick a lot last year; but a man who was out just as much was not fired. Do I have a legal case?

Not necessarily. In one such instance, the New York State Division of Human Rights ruled in favor of the employer. The man had been out for two months, recovered and returned to work; the woman had been out for several days at a time with minor ailments at frequent intervals. The Division agreed with the employer that it was harder for him to cope with the woman's intermittent employment than with the man's single continuous absence for a known period of time.

My employer says that he cannot hire women in one department because the men won't like it. Is this legal?

No. The EEOC guidelines specifically say an employer may not refuse to hire a woman because of the preferences of co-workers.

I'd like to sell our company's products, but I was told that the company won't hire women for selling because the customers would not like it. Is this legal?

No. The EEOC guidelines state that the preferences of customers may *not* be used as a reason for refusing to hire women.

*I was told I'd have to take a special course to qualify for a job
I want, but I've just discovered that the man they hired instead
of me hasn't taken this training at all. Is there anything I can do
about it?*
>   Yes. It's illegal and you can complain to the EEOC.

*Our company distinguishes between "light" and "heavy" jobs
and there are no men in the "light" ones and no women in the
"heavy" ones. Is this legal?*
>   Probably not. The basic principle is that individuals
> must be categorized on their ability to perform, rather
> than on their sex. A woman who can show that she is
> capable of doing so-called "heavy" work cannot be de-
> nied the opportunity simply because she is a woman.

*Until now, the women in our shop have been in a separate job
category, with separate seniority lists. What happens if the lists are
merged?*
>   Back pay may be due the women. The equal oppor-
> tunity laws prohibit dual seniority lines. A bakery work-
> ers' union in Buffalo, New York, in 1972 was ordered to
> pay $1746.40 in compensatory damages to one woman
> because the union maintained separate seniority lists for
> males and females and would not let women work the
> premium-pay night shift.
>   The transition from a dual to a single seniority system
> works hardships on some employees for a while, usually
> the men. Male pursers for the airlines, who were paid
> more than female stewardesses even though both groups
> did similar work, lost their advantage when purser and
> stewardess lists were merged. In the past, a stewardess
> had to give up her seniority if she transferred to the

potentially better-paying job of purser. Since this rule insured that the women would never be promoted over a man, few stewardesses ever applied for the job. Now that the lists are merged, men are forced to compete with women having comparable, or superior, seniority.

However, the battle for equity is not over for the stewardesses. Margaret Maguire, a TWA purser, is suing the airlines for back pay from 1963. She says this is due all the stewardesses who had been illegally denied the promotion and seniority that would have entitled them to qualify for the better-paying job of purser if they had received equal pay from the time they went to work.

Can anyone refuse to hire me because I'm pregnant?

Legally, no. According to a guideline issued by the Equal Employment Opportunity Commission, an employer cannot turn down an applicant just because she is pregnant.

I'm going to have a baby. My company has a policy that no pregnant woman can work after the fifth month, but my doctor says I can work as long as I want to. Can the company force me to leave?

According to the EEOC and an increasing number of union contracts, the disability resulting from pregnancy is a medical decision to be made by a woman and her doctor. Employers, especially school boards, have contended that normal pregnancy interferes with a woman's ability to do the job. Many school administrators feel that a pregnant teacher should not be meeting classes.

There were many court cases involving pregnant

teachers after the passage of the equal opportunity laws, and the legal issue was hotly contested.

What can a pregnant woman do if her employer wants her to quit?

Civil rights lawyers and feminist activists strongly urge pregnant teachers to defy their school boards and rally their colleagues to protest if an attempt is made to make them quit before they wish to.

As employers become more sensitive to the issue, a firm statement that a woman intends to stand on her rights is frequently successful in overturning a previous policy. Clara Bolton succeeded in staying on her job in the purchasing department at Prestolite Electrical Products in Syracuse, New York, beyond the six months that the union contract provided, simply by showing up for work every morning and refusing to leave. After all, what male chauvinist pig will lay hands on a pregnant woman who refuses to budge out of her chair?

Will the company pay me sick leave while I'm out having the baby?

They should if they have a sick leave policy. The EEOC guidelines specifically say that "disabilities caused or contributed to by pregnancy, miscarriage, abortion, childbirth, and recovery therefrom are, for all job-related purposes, temporary disabilities and should be treated as such under any health or temporary disability insurance or sick leave plan available in connection with employment."

State disability insurance plans which fund sick leave in some states are just beginning to offer maternity coverage.

In 1972 five California women and a San Francisco

local of the Waitresses Union filed a class action suit against the director of the California Human Resources Development Department to challenge the state code which, they claimed, expressly denied disability benefits to "alcoholics, drug addicts, and women who are disabled due to pregnancy." Interested groups are beginning to challenge the legality of such exclusions.

If I can't get sick leave, can I collect unemployment insurance for the time I'll be without earnings?

Most states won't give unemployment insurance to a pregnant woman who is laid off, even though she is willing and able to work.

Will the company give me my old job back after the baby is born?

The Equal Employment Opportunity Commission (EEOC) and many court decisions have held that when a woman returns to work after maternity leave, she has to be treated in the same way as any employee who returns after leave for a temporary disability.

I'm not sure now whether I'll want to come back to work after the baby or not. How long can I take to decide?

The terms vary. New York City employees get twelve months' maternity leave, with an extension of another year at the discretion of the agency head. Some organizations allow eighteen months.

My husband wants to stay at home and take care of the baby while I go back to work as soon as possible. Can he get a leave of absence?

It might be possible. "Paternity" or "parental" leave was in the news in the early 1970s. Men were requesting the opportunity to stay home and care for newborn children without losing their jobs, or seniority. Several unions asked for it, and the 1972 City University of New York contract provided for up to twenty days of paid leave and up to eighteen months of unpaid leave for both men and women following the birth of a child.

Will the company medical insurance cover my maternity bills?

Company health insurance plans frequently include maternity expenses, but on a limited basis. However, coverage is being liberalized and extended as women demand that the EEOC policies be enforced, and that pregnancy should not be differentiated from other illnesses.

I'm going to have a baby, but I'm not married. Can I get maternity leave and benefits just the same?

Yes. An employer cannot discriminate against unmarried mothers if he does not discriminate against unmarried fathers.

What about reprisals? Will they take it out on me personally if I file a charge of sex discrimination?

A woman who joins a union, forms a protest committee, files a charge of sex discrimination, or mounts a formal protest of any kind, has to expect that her employer may try to get back at her if he dares. Retaliation is apt to be subtle, however, because all the sex discrimination laws make harassment against complainants a cause for suit itself. The principle comes from the early days of labor unions, when legal protection against union-busting tactics was sought and won.

One of the fastest remedies available to a woman is an injunction under the old National Labor Relations Act which prohibits an employer from firing anyone for organizing in defense of the rights of a group.

When one woman was fired from her clerical job in a major corporation three days after protesting that she was denied a desirable assignment because the boss said he preferred a man in that slot, she complained to her state's human rights agency. The company did not deny the charge and she was reinstated seven weeks later with full back pay for the time out.

She reported that she had no trouble from the men in the office on her return. The boss reported he knew that the company could get into even worse trouble by harassing her. The man who had replaced her was transferred to another department. The only unpleasantness, she said, came from other women in the department, who accused her of being a "Women's Libber."

Can the law against harassment protect me against just plain unpleasantness?

No, it can't. An employer who wants to make life miserable for a woman, or even drive her into nervous breakdown, can usually find a way of doing so that she will find very difficult to prove in court.

The easiest and most common way to get a troublesome woman off the scene is to force her to sit day after day in an empty office with no work. This silent treatment forces the most creative and productive women to resign—which is the whole idea of the harass-

ment. One woman in a government agency was undermined in small ways so badly that she finally had a nervous breakdown and was given a medical discharge.
When another woman filed suit against the same agency
the following year, her boss threatened to sue *her* for
defamation of character. He made her believe that if she
could not prove her charge, she would be guilty of
defaming him by calling him a discriminator.

The employer can also "throw the book" at you, by
enforcing small regulations that are so unreasonable that
they are normally overlooked. This is effective in bureaucracies and is a traditional form of retaliation in the armed
forces.

What happens if you protest these harassments?

Plenty can happen. Lella Smith, a program specialist
in the Department of Justice, got a consent order
through the U.S. District Court, in which the Attorney
General agreed not to harass her, under pain of being
declared in contempt of court—surely a novel and uncomfortable posture for the nation's official lawyer! It
was the first time such an order had been obtained by any
government worker.

The Smith case is a good example of where tit-for-tat
can lead. The case is important because of the precedents it set. In 1971 Lella Smith was a Grade 12 on the
Civil Service scale. She filed a charge of discrimination
through the department's redress machinery because
she said she was doing Grade 15 work without the grade
or pay. Her boss moved her out of her office into a
"broom closet," reassigned her secretary, and ordered
her transferred, on a week's notice, to Columbia, South
Carolina.

Most women would have taken it or quit. Lella Smith decided to fight and hired a lawyer. When reminded by a woman lawyer in the department that harassment was illegal, the Deputy Attorney General countermanded the transfer.

Next day, Ms. Smith's immediate superior tried to transfer her to another section of the department, out of the building. She refused to go until formally ordered in writing.

Her boss then ordered her to pack up her papers and report to the chief of personnel operations. That official disclaimed all knowledge of the order, so Ms. Smith refused to move, whereupon her boss removed her telephone and typewriter.

Ms. Smith then obtained the unprecedented court consent order, under which the Department of Justice agreed to stop harassing her and return her to her duties. She did get her typewriter and secretary back, but no work. About this time the department tribunal ruled that she had really been discriminated against in the first place, so she got the promotion she had demanded as well. But still no duties, even though the court had ordered that she be given her old work back. Instead, her boss gave her a job he himself had neglected to do for six months, and reprimanded her when she could not complete it in four hours. When she went to see her lawyer about this new harassment, the boss charged her with being AWOL.

At this point, Ms. Smith resigned, charging harassment, and requesting a departmental investigation, reinstatement, and suspension of the harassing boss. She returned to court to sue for back pay on her promotion and legal fees.

By this time, of course, the harassment itself had become the major issue and all parties were litigating for the principle of the thing.

Do I have to sue to get an even break on my job? Isn't there something less drastic I can do to get my employer to come to terms with me?

Frequently, just the possibility of a charge is enough to make a company reconsider its policies. In June 1972 the United Parcel Service voluntarily told the EEOC that one out of every four new drivers hired in the Pacific region for the next year would be a woman.

If persuasion fails, and you are involved in an open controversy, you might point out the law that you think has been violated. Barbara Shack, director of the women's rights project of the New York Civil Liberties Union, says that if there's one thing that scares employers more than a lawsuit it is the prospect of appearing in the newspapers as an oppressor of women.

Will the Equal Rights Amendment make any difference to women who work?

The Equal Rights Amendment to the U.S. Constitution provides that "Equality of rights under the law shall not be abridged by the United States or by any State on account of sex." Lawyers who oppose the amendment have argued that the legal disabilities of women are being removed so rapidly that the amendment is not needed. Feminists want the amendment to become law not only because of its moral assertion of equality, but because it removes a parcel of annoying little inequities that are presently being attacked through the slow and expensive process of pushing test cases up to the Supreme Court of the United States.

It provides instant and unequivocal equality in employment. Men and women will get equal Social Security benefits and at the same ages. A widower will collect benefits earned by his deceased wife's work on the same basis that a widow collects from the credits earned by her deceased husband. The amendment will end differentials in government pensions on the basis of sex, which in some instances have left women with smaller pensions than men. And it means an end to the state laws "protecting" women workers by limiting their hours, the weights they may lift, and their duties, which have been used as an excuse to keep women out of some high-paying jobs.

The Equal Rights Amendment removes the legal disabilities that in some states still limit the freedom of married women to sign contracts and go into business on the same basis as men. Married women will find it easier to borrow money on their own when husbands are no more responsible for the debts of wives than wives are responsible for the debts of husbands. All these discriminatory policies have been on the way out, but ERA would kill them off at a single blow.

12

Collective Action: Unions and Caucuses

My husband's a strong union man—and he's often said that if it wasn't for the union, he wouldn't be making as much money as he is now. Do you think unions could help women also?

They are already doing so. In 1970 union women who worked full time all year earned $452 a year more than women who didn't belong to a union, according to a study made by the Bureau of Labor Statistics. Unions are the main reasons why teachers and government workers are earning more than they used to. A 1972 study made by the Tax Foundation credits the American Federation of State, County and Municipal Employees and other unions of government employees with helping to boost government payrolls 88 percent between 1960 and 1970.

They're trying to form a union in my office, but so far I've steered clear of it. Do I have anything to gain by joining?

Better investigate before you say no. A woman typist in her sixties who thought that unions were for factory workers changed her mind in a hurry when she discovered that she needed $1,000 worth of work on her teeth and that this dental work would be covered under the union medical plan. Unions offer inexpensive medical and life insurance, charter flights, college scholarships for your children, and, in some cases, even child care.

I don't know any women who do belong to unions. Aren't unions only for people who work in factories?

Many white-collar workers are now union women. In 1972 nearly 80,000 women teachers belonged to the National Education Association, a professional society that now functions as a teachers' union. It had more members than all the clothing unions, which have always had large numbers of women members. Another 300,-000 women belonged to the burgeoning American Federation of State, County and Municipal Employees.

But aren't unions really for men?

It seems that way because unions are stronger in the crafts and factory jobs where men predominate. Only one woman worker out of seven is a union member compared with three out of ten males. But the unionization of teachers and government workers is increasing this percentage. More than 4 million women belonged to unions in 1970, an increase of 342,000 over 1968.

Could unions do anything for secretaries?

Secretaries are beginning to hold indignation meet-ings, and some of these go on to the logical step of unionization. Margie Albert, a legal secretary, was so encouraged by the gains made through organizing the secretaries in the New York law firm where she worked that she gave up her ambitions to become a lawyer and is devoting herself to the unionization of office workers instead. She got started when women lawyers sought to raise the consciousness of all the women in the firm, professional and clerical, through a series of meetings. The secretaries began to see that they were catering to their bosses in ways that went beyond simply doing the job. "We ran errands, handled personal matters, served lunches," Ms. Albert says. "Sometimes we were treated as though we were inanimate objects, like the machines we operated. Often we were excluded, as though invisi-ble, from interesting discussions among the attorneys about the cases they (and we) were working on."

As the secretaries talked, they began to realize that they were put down because of their status as well as because they were women. "The cost of living was rising and we needed more money. We weren't happy with our vacations or medical coverage or sick leave, and we wanted some provision for our future—a pension plan or severance pay."

The upshot was that the secretaries decided to organ-ize. They broke off from the professional women who had started the discussions and shopped around for a union. An officer from District 65 of the National Coun-cil of Distributive Workers of America assisted them in organizing and negotiating with their employer.

Their first contract scored important gains. They defeated the management concept of a "limit" to office workers' pay, and one of the secretaries in the firm now makes more than $300 a week. They have won the right to "personal days" off, so that they don't have to lie about being sick when they need a day off for tending to important personal matters.

Other new benefits they gained included a grievance procedure, complete medical coverage for themselves and their families, severance pay, and annual cost-of-living increases along with salary increments.

I've heard that unions aren't very helpful on women's rights issues. Is that true?

Some are, some aren't. And you can't go by the percentage of women in the membership. Two of the most progressive unions, as far as women's rights are concerned, are the United Auto Workers (UAW), and the International Union of Electrical, Radio and Machine Workers (IUE), in which women are a minority. On the other hand, unions with a large percentage of women, the International Ladies Garment Workers Union (ILGWU), 80 percent female; the Amalgamated Clothing Workers of America (ACW), 75 percent female; and the Communications Workers of America (CWA), 55 percent female, have, in the past, condoned industry practices that reserve some of the better-paying jobs for men. Many women teachers fault both the conservative National Education Association and the more militant American Federation of Teachers, both of which have a majority of women members, with dragging their feet on demands of special concern to their women members.

Why have unions been so slow to protect their women members?

Because the first unions in this country were dominated by men, who were afraid that employers would bring in women to cut wages. That's why they originally set up separate seniority and pay schedules for men and women. They have also been in favor of state laws "protecting" women against overtime and heavy lifting because they have been able to use these supposed differences in capability to justify higher pay for men.

Then, too, the first unions had so few women that it was easy to ignore their wishes and, when something had to give at the bargaining table, to drop demands for maternity leave, day-care centers, and a fair shake on fringe benefits.

Hasn't anybody told unions about Women's Liberation?

Indeed they have. Some unions have had a dedicated core of feminists boring from within for decades. One of these is the United Auto Workers Union, which has long maintained an aggressive women's division. It was the first union to come out for the Equal Rights Amendment, and declare its opposition to state protective laws that keep women out of the overtime and supervisory jobs.

But have unions been doing anything for their women members lately?

"Unions are eliminating sex classifications and are using job descriptions to determine pay," according to Barbara Wertheimer, labor program specialist at Cornell University's School of Industrial and Labor Relations.

District Council 37 with the assistance of the American

Federation of State, County and Municipal Workers, and
its local union of custodial assistants in New York City
recently reached an agreement with the city to do away
with separate pay and duty rolls for men and women.
Jobs are now defined by description and are available to
persons of either sex who demonstrate that they can
perform the duties required. The contract has been approved by the National Pay Board.

A company far from Appalachia launched a campaign
to recruit 1,000 men there for new jobs it was creating,
without first attempting to recruit from the large number
of women who already lived within commuting distance
of the plant. The jobs in question paid $4.50 an hour, far
more than most women could earn on a "woman's job"
in that community. The United Auto Workers, with its
strong women's division, was able to achieve a shift in
the company's recruitment policies, and as a result many
local women began taking home the fattest paychecks of
their lives.

In another case, UAW pressured a company to retain
more than 100 women employees with thirty years of
service when it moved its plant to a new location just a
few miles away. Without the intercession of the UAW,
the women would have lost their jobs and would have
had to settle for reduced pensions, if indeed they had
invested enough years and had reached the required age
for retirement benefits.

*Can a union help a woman who is discriminated against in pay
on the basis of sex?*

Although few union contracts bind employers not to
discriminate on the basis of sex, many of the grievances
of women employees could be handled by unions
through existing, traditional grievance machinery if the

union steward and local were sympathetic. And union machinery has the advantage of protecting a union member against retaliation.

"The union has a duty to take sex discrimination grievances to arbitration," according to Ruth Weyand, a lawyer with the International Union of Electrical, Radio and Machine Workers (IUE). She points out that a local union has the right to approve or disapprove the arbitrators who sit individually or on a panel to hear such cases, and it could use this right of approval to screen out arbitrators who might not treat a charge of sex discrimination fairly. Ms. Weyand often recommends names of sympathetic arbitrators to locals that request them. She suggests that compiling and distributing a list of arbitrators versed in sex discrimination would be a worthwhile project for a women's group.

Barbara Wertheimer, labor-program specialist at Cornell University's School of Industrial and Labor Relations, says: "Women going into unionized jobs have an obligation to use union grievance machinery, the logical channel, before resorting to other channels for redress." She feels that trying to go around the established grievance structure will only stir up antagonisms.

"Start with your union first when you have a grievance," she advises. "The first thing they'll ask at EEOC is 'Have you reported this to your union?' "

A woman owes it to herself, Ms. Wertheimer points out, to know the channels of grievance procedure, to study the union contract history, union structure, and union history itself.

But what if the union won't do anything to help a woman claiming job discrimination?

A woman who is ignored by her union, despite all

her efforts, should kick until she is heard. She can and should complain to her shop steward, the president of her local, and right on up the line to the head of her union. She should attend union meetings and speak up. As a starter, she might cite the finding of the EEOC that a union *can* bring a charge of sex discrimination on behalf of a member even if that very same union signed a contract that was discriminatory. Courts will not enforce an illegal provision of a contract, and a 1971 decision expressly states that a complainant need not come into court "with clean hands."

If the union balks, a woman member might also point out that she has a right to sue the union for conniving in illegal discrimination. Hundreds of such charges have already been brought against reluctant unions.

What can women do to make their unions more responsive?

They can participate in union affairs. Union officers complain that women make poor union members. When they don't go to meetings, and don't work for the union, it's easy to ignore them.

It is good politics for a woman to shoulder her share of the responsibility for union activities and to become accepted before trying to bring about change.

"Unions are political organizations," explains Valerie Howard, director of women's activities for the Communications Workers of America. "They push in areas where there is political pressure on them. Up to now, women have not exerted this pressure." The union will begin to respond to them when they use its machinery more effectively, when they participate, petition, do committee work, and run for union office.

Do unions discriminate against women within the unions themselves?

A great many women union members say so. Men monopolize the top jobs even in those unions where the majority of the members are women, such as the clothing workers' unions. Charlotte Hallam, staff associate in the teacher rights' division of the National Education Association (NEA) complains that there are only a "couple" of women on NEA's field service staff. To remedy this inequity, women employed by unions are forming their own caucuses and making their own demands against the union that employs them. In some cases, they have even threatened to strike the union.

Even if all a union's members are women, wouldn't they be better off with a man heading them and doing their negotiating for them?

It hasn't worked out that way. The airline stewardesses were never successful in achieving recognition of their demands until they parted company from the airline pilots' union. They broke away from the Air Line Pilots Association in 1963 and formed the Airline Stewards and Stewardesses Association as part of the Transport Workers Union. They contended that "the only thing in common between stewardesses and pilots is that they go up in airplanes."

The conflict dates from the earliest days of flying. Pilots were opposed to stewardesses when the first six of them, all registered nurses, first went aloft back in 1930. "The pilots didn't want us at all," recalled Inez Keller Fuite of San Diego, one of the original group. "They were rugged, temperamental characters who wore guns to protect the mail. They wouldn't even speak to us during the first couple of trips." Wives of pilots even wrote the airline asking that the stewardesses be removed.

With their own union, stewardesses have been able to push up wages and end many onerous discriminations against them. They won the right to work after marriage, even after motherhood, and are no longer required to retire or take ground jobs at thirty-two or thirty-five.

But it hasn't always been easy. When Margaret Maguire was a TWA stewardess, she wanted to fight the company's policy of limiting the purser's job to men, not only because the pursers earned more, but because only pursers could move up the promotional ladder to become service managers, a job that can pay $16,000 a year.

The TWA contract with the Airline Stewards and Stewardesses provided for hostesses (all female) who served food and drink on the airplane and were trained in emergency procedures according to FAA regulations, and it provided for pursers (all male), who did exactly the same thing except that on international flights the pursers also passed out customs declarations to passengers and took care of international papers for the crew and cargo. This additional paperwork is so simple that when Ms. Maguire was finally made a purser, she discovered that the purser training school in Kansas City simply provided stewardess training, and the additional paperwork required only five minutes to master.

The big difference between the jobs is pay. The pursers' salary scale *begins* at a higher figure than the *top* pay any hostess can earn, and then moves up with seniority. If there were a real difference in the jobs, and the purser's job required more responsibility, it would be logical for the hostesses to move up into the purser category.

But in practice, no stewardess had ever been made a purser before June 1968, when Ms. Maguire complained to two Federal agencies that the airline's policies were discriminatory. No particular reason was given for this, except the circular one that since no women did the job, there must be something unfeminine about it. And since most of the stewardesses used to quit to marry, few of them had the seniority to challenge their exclusion. Stewardesses reached the top of the hostess seniority list after eight years. Margaret Maguire had had 15 years as a hostess and could feel the ceiling. After five years, a male purser was making $2,500 more than a female hostess earned after eight years.

Back in 1967, Ms. Maguire asked the union to do something about what appeared to her (and has since been adjudicated to be) a clear violation of the Equal Pay Act of 1963. Until the middle 1960s, companies could get around the act simply by giving the men who did the job a different title. And, if it had not been for women like Margaret Maguire, that's the way it would still be now.

The union said, "No. We don't want to open up a can of worms." The two categories, purser and hostess, were embedded in their contracts. And the company could easily plead the contract as a defense against the Equal Pay Act. The union itself would have had to be a defendant.

Margaret Maguire then campaigned for union office. During the campaign, she soft-pedaled the women's issues she really wanted the union to press. She concealed her membership in the National Organization for Women. Although union membership protected her from personal retaliation from the company, exposing her only to ridicule intended to scare away more timid women (and in part succeeding), she had no protection from the disapproval of other women, although they have since been very glad to take advantage of the rights and pay she has won them.

She instituted a formal complaint in 1968, when most sex-discrimination cases were moving very slowly. Ms. Maguire believes that the only reason she was able to get fast action was because of her union activity, and because she filed her charge with the Office of Federal Contract Compliance as well as the Equal Employment Opportunity Commission. She got everything she wanted in 1970 via a union contract, except for back pay, and she sued for that later on.

She believes that unions have not always worked for women because the women themselves have not demanded it. When they do, it works.

What if there isn't a union in my shop?

Consider organizing one, especially if your pay is less than union scale. Women wishing to organize locals must be careful to follow procedures prescribed under the Taft-Hartley Act, which covers all jobs except those held by farm, household, and supervisory workers. A union must be certified by the National Labor Relations Board before it can be recognized by an employer as the bona fide representative for a particular group of workers. Anyone interested in organizing a local in her place of employment should call or write the organizing department of an appropriate national or international union for guidance.

"Those who have accepted 'women's roles' by going into jobs 'appropriate' for women, such as secretaries and teachers, are the most difficult to unionize," according to Catherine East, executive secretary of the Citizens' Advisory Council on the Status of Women. Part of the problem, says Ms. East, is that in the past, unions have not used women to organize women. They have used not only the same techniques as they use with male workers, but also the same male organizers to organize women.

Unions are not always the answer. Can women improve their job situations by joining with other women in other ways?

Yes. Superior and determined individuals have always succeeded in beating a system that keeps them down, but the only way to change the system itself is through collective action. Informal women's groups, and more formal women's caucuses have sprung up all across the country in offices and factories, in large cities and small towns, as women realize how much more they can do together.

And as pointed out earlier, equal opportunity specialists invariably urge collective action to fight employment discrimination legally. Just as a hundred names on a petition are more impressive to the front office than a single letter of complaint, a long list of names in a class-action suit is more impressive to the court—and far safer for each individual.

What kinds of collective action have worked for women?

The most important collective action has, of course, been the women's equality movement that began in 1966 with the formation of the National Organization for Women (NOW). As in the World War I fight for suffrage, the activists and organizers of the movement have been a pitiably small minority, subjected to ridicule not only by the press and by men, but by large numbers of apathetic women. Like the suffragists, the contemporary activists for sex equality have made up in militance what they have lacked in numbers. Their demonstrations, protests, studies, lobbying, and above all, their willingness to brave public opinion are directly responsible for the growing body of antidiscrimination laws. These laws have improved pay and job opportunities for a "minority" that differs from the blacks, the Jews, the Chicanos, and the foreign-born because it comprises 51 percent of the population. Seldom have so many owed so much to so few.

The women's movement has done a lot for women workers in general, and deserves support on that basis, but will it do me any good personally to join? Won't my boss think I'm a troublemaker if I join NOW?

Every woman has to make her own decision about how active she wishes to be in any group effort. Like her politics or her religion, a woman's orientation to the women's movement is her own business and need not come up in job interviews or in her working relationship unless she wishes. She may choose to ignore direct putdowns, profiting as best she can from the general improvement the movement has spearheaded, or she may wish to become part of the movement by asserting her rights on her own job. She may choose merely to remind her employer of antidiscrimination laws he may be violating, or go to the extreme of making herself a test case.

The attitude a woman takes is largely a matter of personal style. Many women are suspicious of anything that smacks of "Women's Lib," and most of those who have already made it into really important management positions advise young women to deal casually and even humorously with day-to-day sex discrimination. They have a good point. It is hard to move ahead while feeling constantly victimized. The other side of the coin is that it is very hard to do what is necessary to get paid what you are worth if you refuse to recognize that you *are not* paid what you're worth. Though painful, "consciousness raising" is the first step toward equality.

How can the women's organizations help me on my job?

They can help you and other women on your job organize to change some of the working conditions that keep you down.

Individual women have profited from the movement in a variety of ways. Some have gained valuable self-confidence. Others have moved ahead in their work because of the exposure the movement has given them. Many early militants have gone into trade-union work or become equal opportunity officers, leaders in the new industry created by equal opportunity legislation. Pressure to promote women from organized women's groups has resulted in the discovery and promotion of hundreds, perhaps thousands of women who would otherwise be living out their working days in ill-paid, invisible backroom jobs.

I can't imagine the women in our department organizing by themselves. Aren't most groups started by outside agitatiors?

No. They spring up around very specific job grievances—the kind of trivial but wounding indignities that sparked the formation of many unions and wildcat, or unauthorized, strikes.

A good example is what happened at the Group

Health Association of America, in Washington. One of the secretaries complained to Nancy Perlman, then assistant to the director of education and training, that she was afraid of getting fired if she did not do personal work for her boss. Nancy suggested that all the office women get together and compare notes. At the meeting, it developed that secretaries were addressing personal Christmas cards, picking up shirts at the laundry for their bosses on Saturdays, and doing personal typing, often after hours. Since the chores were not office work, they felt they should not put in overtime.

As the women talked, they began to see that personnel policies didn't spell out what was expected of them. They formed a committee, drew up six recommendations, and presented them to the executive director. Though surprised, and nettled, he agreed to three of them, but when Ms. Perlman later reproached him for filling a job without posting the vacancy as promised, the director of education and training told her that she had no business meddling in the management of the secretaries. When the women rallied to her support, he fired her for "making trouble." On advice of counsel, she complained that very day to the National Labor Relations Board, which took prompt action against the Group Health Association under its power to enjoin an employer from firing an employee for collective action.

The experience converted Ms. Perlman into a professional union worker. She is now employed by the American Federation of State, County and Municipal Workers.

Are there many women's action groups of that kind?

Barbara Hirst, a candidate for a master's degree in manpower development at the New School for Social Research, counted at least 100 such groups in American businesses, foundations, universities, unions, and government agencies in 1972. Without doing extensive research, she uncovered informal, ad hoc women's action groups at *Time, Newsweek,* Polaroid, Atlantic Richfield, General Electric, Scott Foresmen, *Reader's Digest,* Celanese, the Ford Foundation, CARE, the Rand Corporation, AT&T, Pitney-Bowes, the Museum of Modern Art in New York City, Blue Cross, and all three national broadcasting networks.

Why are there caucuses in those well-known organizations and firms? They can't be as bad as the places I know about where women are really kept down.

The groups are most apt to form in organizations with a social conscience, where awareness of the women's movement is high both on the part of the management and the employees. The existence of a women's group may mean that conditions are improving, but not fast enough to satisfy the most ambitious women.

Are all the women's groups offshoots of the Women's Liberation Movement?

In a general sense, they grow out of a climate of concern for sex equality. Barbara Hirst, who researched them, found that the most successful groups were those that were getting advice and research help from feminist organizations, but most of them were not founded to proselytize for the movement. According to Ms. Hirst, they usually began with "very low-key groups concerned with nonexplosive issues, small grievances, poor attitude, and lack of consideration on the part of predominantly male bosses."

What do these women's employee groups want?

They want what blacks and other minorities want: decent working conditions, "respect," and a say in their own work. Grievance procedures and formal personnel policies on hiring, firing, promotion, and posting of job vacancies are frequent objectives. Open discussion about affirmative action programs was a very popular goal in 1972. In addition, most groups asked for career ladders for *all* jobs, particularly the dead-end secretarial posts held by women, the inclusion of women in apprenticeship and management training programs, review of the credentials of women already employed who might have been ignored in promotions, paid maternity leave, and provisions for child care.

Why don't dissatisfied women employees just form a union and be done with it?

Grievance procedures, job posting, and formal personnel policies are the classic first demands of unions, it is true. But Ms. Hirst, in a study of caucuses, found that many of the women in these groups are violently anti-union. Like most middle-class women, they think unions are for factory workers. And like the Group Health Association committee, most of them are formed and led by professional or administrative women who are finding their aspirations thwarted by the gold-plated ghetto that supposedly enlightened organizations create for bright women.

The widely publicized "revolt" of underpaid women at the *Reader's Digest* was started by women with relatively good jobs in editorial or advertising work who discovered that men were getting paid twice as much as women for the same kind of work. In 1972 several dozen *Digest* women at all levels filed a class action complaint with the Equal Employment Opportunity Commission. The charge attracted nationwide attention when some of the women publicized conditions in the large subscription department of clerical workers who at times had been under surveillance by closed-circuit television, and required to ask permission to go to the toilet, like children in school. Management responded by promoting many women—in title at least—including five to the level of senior editor.

Have women's caucuses or employee organizations accomplished anything tangible for the women employed in them?

Results have occasionally been dramatic. At the Ford Foundation, for instance, which has been described as a "country club" of working conditions, a women's caucus resulted in pay raises for fourteen women in what one member described as the "neitherland" status—neither professional nor support staff. Some months later, management adopted the policy of posting job openings so that women in support positions could apply for them.

A petition signed by almost all women employees of the *Washington Post* asked management to recruit more women professionals, give them more important assignments and review sexist handling of news items. This opened talks with the newspaper's management and resulted in a promise to expand the role of newswomen in top- and middle-management positions.

Other groups have succeeded in getting employers to admit women to training programs, and even those with few tangible achievements have raised the consciousness of employers. Many have gathered statistical evidence of the discrimination against women in the organization for presentation to government inspectors checking the equal employment practices required of government contractors.

Some, like the Alliance for Women at the telephone company, and the groups in several Federal agencies, work cooperatively with management-sponsored women's groups that are assigned to implement affirmative action plans.

Okay, maybe we ought to have a women's group in our shop. How should I go about forming one?

Most of the groups start with an indignation meeting of three or four women who are upset over a specific grievance. They talk to other employees and a meeting is held at someone's home. Nancy Nesewich, who helped to organize women in the Chicago headquarters of Blue Cross, agrees with Margie Albert, who has been working to unionize secretaries, that it is important to start with nonideological, "bread and butter" grievances, so as not to alienate those women who fear association with "Women's Lib."

A solid project is important to sustain interest. For instance, the Blue Cross group has conducted an exhaustive survey of the jobs held by women in that organization. Indignation can flare quickly over a specific issue, but may die again just as quickly once the grievance is redressed. That happened when all the women workers at the Sands Point, New York, plant of IBM staged a one-day protest against a company prohibition that forbid women to wear pants to work. Management quietly capitulated, and the revolt was over, as was the indignation.

Important decisions should be made early in a group's

existence. Who is eligible? Should women bosses be included? Some of the most effective groups have cut
across rank lines, in keeping with the new feminist doctrine of sisterhood. How militant does the group want to
be? Should the group confine itself to gathering facts
and counseling individual women on their legal rights,
or should it start a "zap" action such as the media women
launched against the *Ladies' Home Journal,* with national
television coverage, in 1970? The groups that are industry-wide have another problem: how far can women in
competing firms go in exchanging information that their
bosses might consider trade secrets?

The caucuses which have been most successful in win-
ning their demands were those that cooperated with
company officials. And in order to keep attention for-
cused on goals, most of the caucuses report that they
have had to go into consciousness-raising.

*Isn't there a danger that a woman who organizes one of these
groups will be fired?*

The danger is real. Most managers are indignant at
the very idea of a secretarial revolt. They think that they
treat their women well and put the organizers down as
victims of "Women's Lib" or "bad apples." At Lawyers
Publishing, in Rochester, New York, a woman supervisor
told her superiors that the women were not allowed the
coffee breaks given to men. Management asked, "Who's
complaining?" When she refused to single out any one
woman for purge, she was fired herself, and then sued
the company both for discrimination and retaliation.

Gayle Lubin, a topless go-go dancer in a Washington,
D.C., restaurant, was involved in a similar case. Normally
four girls took turns, dancing fifteen minutes and resting

forty-five minutes. When one girl was missing, three danced twenty minutes each and rested forty. When only two girls were present, each one danced thirty minutes and rested thirty minutes but without extra pay. When the last situation became frequent, Ms. Lubin proposed that the absent third girl's pay be divided between the two who performed. Her employer accused her of trying to start a union and said: "I don't want any troublemakers around here. You are fired."

Ms. Lubin protested to the National Labor Relations Board, which ruled that she had been engaged in "protected concerted activity" and had been discharged illegally. She was awarded back pay at $30 a day, totaling around $1,000, and reinstatement in her job, although she elected to stay with a new employer.

"I wasn't trying to start a union when they fired me," she said, "but I think it's a good idea now."

Would a women's caucus in our organization help all those women who are always grumbling to each other? Would it be good for morale?

Many observers think that the impact of women's caucuses on morale and self-confidence is their most important achievement.

Sociology departments in graduate schools were among the first organizations in which women's caucuses arose. At the University of California, Berkeley, the dropout rate of women graduate students in sociology during the first three years of graduate school was 70 percent for women who entered from 1961 to 1964. The dropout rate fell to 33 percent for women entering from 1968 to 1970. The dropout rate for men fell from 42 percent in the early period to 36 percent, higher than the dropout rate for women in the same year. In a doctoral dissertation, Lucy W. Sells suggests that the presence of a caucus was responsible for more women completing their work.

What other groups can a woman join to improve her working conditions?

Professional women's groups and industry-wide caucuses have been formed to promote the status of women in their fields. In addition to the well-organized women's caucuses in the academic disciplines, such as the Ad Hoc Committee on the Status of Women in Sociology (see resource section for listing of other groups), there are industry-wide groups, such as the National Association of Media Women, and professional groups, such as the Women's Caucus of the National Lawyers Guild, and Federally Employed Women.

Won't women lose more than they gain by antagonizing male employers?

There may be temporary setbacks for some militant individuals—but temporary is the important word. And there is a fine line to be drawn between what one woman can accomplish to upgrade women generally, and what she does that will hurt, or help, her own career.

At a meeting of women legislators, Senator Clara Weisenborn, a Republican who has been in the Ohio legislature for eighteen years, said that women in state legislatures all over the country "are not privileged to know the mechanics that are going on in the inner circle because we are not committee chairmen." She went on to point out that the general lack of leadership positions for women was probably their own fault "because we're not pushing." She added, "There isn't a single solitary door in this world that will open without pushing. I've always refused to acknowledge a closed door." Senator Weisenborn went back to Ohio, got herself re-elected to the Ohio legislature, and less than a year later, she was appointed chairman of the Education, Health, and Welfare Committee—the first time a woman has ever held a chairmanship in the Ohio Senate.

And when women band together, the doors open more easily. The National Women's Political Caucus succeeded in getting both the Republican and Democratic parties to move some women into important party positions.

As more women enter the job market, isn't the "ghetto" segregation of jobs by sex breaking down?

No, it is getting worse because the ghetto jobs are the easiest ones to get. As more women work, the women's job ghetto becomes even larger, and harder to escape from.

Women are going to work faster than sex barriers are being removed, and the pay gap has actually increased during the last fifteen years. In 1955, when 36 percent of all women over sixteen were in the labor force, the median income of women working full time was 64 percent that of men. In 1971, when more than 43 percent were in the labor force, their median income had dropped to 59 percent that of men.

What do women do who need more money?

Many of them hold second jobs. More than 760,000 women were among the four million "moonlighters"—

people with two or more jobs—during 1971. In spite of rising unemployment, 130,000 more women moonlighted than in 1970, but the number of males who moonlighted stayed the same. Most of the women with two jobs were between twenty-five and thirty-four years old, and many were single, divorced, or widows who needed the money. They were mostly clerks, health workers, teachers, factory operators, and service workers such as waitresses. Almost half were in the service industries and finance. For 90 percent of these women, the second job added less than $50 a week to their incomes.

Ghetto jobs force the rising proportion of those women who are on their own to take a second job to make both ends meet.

Do women suffer more than men in a recession when jobs are tight?

Not any more than they always do. During the recession of 1971-1972, policies for upgrading women seemed to have slowed down because of budget cuts and freezes on hiring. Women began to suspect that, like blacks, they were "first fired and last hired." But it's not quite that simple.

Unemployment rates are always high for women because, like blacks, they have the jobs that do not carry tenure, and are concentrated at the bottom where turnover is high. But the unemployment rate for women did not rise faster than that of men during the recession period.

This was also true in the Great Depression of the 1930s. Then, as now, women were more apt to have salaried jobs, which held up better through hard times than the hourly work that men did. Jobs were so sex-segregated that employers could not find men trained to do the work of women typists, nurses, and teachers, however much they would have liked to fire women and give their jobs to men. And whenever employers could choose, women worked for less money.

In hard times, women who are overqualified become an irresistible employment bargain. In 1970 and 1971 many firms hired as many or more women college graduates as they did in the past, while cutting down on the men. In rejuggling work assignments, budget cutters frequently find that a woman with a lower title, such as assistant or clerk, can do work that in more flush times would go to a promotable young man or junior executive if the firm contemplated expansion.

The well-known fact that women produce more per dollar of pay works for them during economic slowdowns, but it also reinforces the ghetto walls. Like blacks, women get a chance to move out of limited jobs when business is expanding. A standstill or a cutback makes it hard to correct inequities painlessly.

When employment figures begin to rise, as they did after the recession of 1971–1972, doesn't that mean more jobs for everybody, including women?

It depends on whose employment is being counted. In the past, the Federal government has publicized unemployment figures on the basis of "married men who are heads of families." Women who are heads of families, many of whom are black, are so frequently out of work, that the unemployment rate is much higher when it is quoted in terms of "heads of family" of both sexes.

Aren't things going to get better for women? Aren't more nonghetto jobs opening up all the time?

Yes, for individual women—but the Labor Department manpower forecasts for the decade ahead say that the biggest percentage increase in jobs will be in the limited ranks of professional, technical, and executive workers. Only a small number of women will benefit from these. Jobs in service occupations are also expected to grow rapidly, but many of these are low-paying jobs, such as waitresses, stewardesses, household workers, and hospital attendants. For women without a college education, they are the heart of the ghetto.

The outlook is for a bigger, if not a better employment ghetto for the average woman. And she won't get paid what she's worth until and unless she takes the initiative to break out of it.

Resource Section

DOCUMENTING DISCRIMINATION

The inferior employment status of women has been and is being documented by an authoritative and growing volume of literature, both scholarly and activist. Anyone who thinks women *are* being paid what they're worth, or who needs evidence of the many ways in which women are kept down on the job should spend a few minutes with one of the following books:

Handbook on Women Workers 1969, Wage and Labor Standards Adminstration, U.S. Department of Labor, Washington, D.C. This is the Bible, with cold facts, laws, and statistics. It has a good bibliography of books and organizations. Available from the Superintendent of Documents, U.S. Government Printing Office, Washington, D.C. 20402, for $1.50.

Born Female: The High Cost of Keeping Women Down, by Caroline Bird, with Sara Welles Briller. David McKay and Pocketbooks, New York, 1968: revised edition, 1970. A reporter's presentation of the facts of discrimination; used as a text for many women's studies programs.

Woman's Place: Options and Limits in Professional Careers, by Cynthia Fuchs Epstein. University of California Press, Berkeley, 1970. A penetrating analysis by a professional sociologist.

Sex in the Marketplace: American Women at Work, by Juanita M. Kreps. Johns Hopkins Press, Baltimore, 1971. An authoritative economic analysis of the labor-force participation of American women that documents their underutilization.

The Women's Bureau of the Department of Labor also issues periodic fact sheets on the labor-force participation of women, working mothers, the earnings gap between men and women, and "Why Women Work." For a full listing, write for "Publications of the Women's Bureau," Superintendent of Documents, U.S. Government Printing Office, Washington, D.C. 20402.

Bibliographies are a fast guide to the voluminous literature on the employment of women, studies of motivation and behavior on the job, and many investigations of the role of women in specific occupations:

Women: A Bibliography on Their Education and Careers, by Helen S. Astin, Nancy Suniewick, and Susan Dweck. Sponsored by University Research Corporation and the Institute of Life Insurance, Human Service Press, 4301 Connecticut Avenue NW, Washington, D.C., 1971.

Women's Work and Women's Studies, by Kirsten Drake, Dorothy Marks, and Mary Wexford, The Women's Center, Barnard College, 1971. Published by KNOW Inc., P.O. Box 86031, Pittsburgh, Pennsylvania 15221. Mimeographed; 1,445 entries for the year 1971 alone. $4.50, prepaid.

Women's Studies Abstracts, P.O. Box 1, Rush, New York 14543. A quarterly, giving the gist of several hundred articles in each issue.

Newsletters: Laws, practices, and attitudes are changing so fast that anyone who wants to keep up with the battle against sex discrimination needs at least one of the newsletters in the general area:

The Spokeswoman, owned and edited by Susan Davis, 5464 South Shore Drive, Chicago, Illinois 60615. A monthly summary of current events on issues important to women, with horizen-widening "help wanted" ads listing high-paying professional and executive job openings. $7 a year to individuals, $12 for institutions.

Women Today, published by Myra Barrer, Today Publications, 621 National Press Building, Washington, D.C. 20004. A biweekly six-page letter reporting news of employment, education, laws, and court cases. Authoritative about the Washington scene. $15 a year. (Includes subscription to monthly WEAL *Washington Reports,* which follows the status of national legislation that affects women.)

Womanpower: A Monthly Report on Fair Employment Practices for Women, edited and published by Betsy Hogan, Betsy Hogan Associates, 222 Rawson Road, Brookline, Massachusetts 02146. A monthly newsletter on laws, regulations, and trends that affect the status of women in the work force. Edited for employers, managers, and supervisors, but just as useful for the working women affected.

Educational Organizations: Reports, guides, and pamphlets available on request or at a modest fee are a principal product of public and private organizations promoting the status of women.

For up-to-date information on specific aspects of discrimination, write: Citizens' Advisory Council on the Status of Women, Josephine Gutwillig, chairman; Catherine East, executive secretary, U.S. Department of Labor, Washington, D.C. The Council makes an annual report of progress on equal rights, maternity leave, part-time employment, and other issues.

The National Federation of Business and Professional Women's Clubs, 2012 Massachusetts Avenue NW, Washington, D.C. 20036. Though conservative by present-day standards, the BPW was in there fighting for women's employment rights long before Women's Liberation.

The National Organization for Women (NOW), 1957 East 73rd Street, Chicago, Illinois 60649. NOW, with its hundreds of chapters all over the country, takes action on all women's rights. The NOW Compliance Task Force works to change laws, policies and regulations pertaining to women's employment. Local chapters try to be helpful to individual women who have specific employment problems. Because it is volunteer staffed, services and information vary with times and places.

Barnard Women's Center, Barnard College, Broadway

at 117th Street, New York, N.Y. 10027. A clearing-house of information for women in the New York City area. The Center publishes *Women's Work and Women's Studies,* an annual research bibliography, distributes free a "Reading Guide to the New Feminism," and maintains a library of articles and books on women.

Women's History Library, 2325 Oak Street, Berkeley, California 94708. A fascinating collection of feminist books and pamphlets well worth a visit—and a donation. They will search files on specific topics for a fee.

CHOOSING A VOCATION

Women are underpaid in part because they are more apt than men to accept whatever job turns up. Getting into the right occupation in the first place improves a woman's chance of getting paid what she is worth.

Books and Pamphlets: Any woman planning a career should consult the *Occupational Outlook Handbook,* U.S. Department of Labor Bulletin 1700, available in most libraries. Nearly 900 pages of information on every conceivable occupation, such as preparation required, numbers of persons in the occupation, pay ranges, and outlook. Five minutes spent looking up the occupation of your choice in this encyclopedia is worth hours of soul-searching. Check, also, the less formidable quarterly supplements for the most recent trends in occupations.

Careers for Women, Women's Bureau, U.S. Department of Labor. The Women's Bureau issues a series of pamphlets on specific careers. Reports have been available on engineering, mathematics, medical technology, optometry, personnel, pharmacy, public relations, technical writing, urban planning, and apprenticeships. Available through U.S. Government Printing Office, Washington, D.C. 20402.

Career Counseling: New Perspectives for Women and Girls, A Selected Annotated Bibliography, Business and Professional Women's Foundation, 2012 Massachusetts Avenue NW, Washington, D.C. 20036, 1972. A useful guide to the recent vocational-guidance literature, available for $.50 if your local library doesn't have it.

Careers for College Women, A Bibliography of Vocational Materials, selected by Georgia P. Watermulder, the University of Michigan Center for Continuing Education of Women, 330 Thompson Street, Ann Arbor, Michigan 48108, January 1968. Older, but useful because it breaks the literature down into occupations of special interest to college women such as "travel agency" and "city planning."

Career Opportunity Series, by Catalyst, 6 East 82nd Street, New York, New York 10028. Booklets available at $.95 each on careers in accounting, advertising, art, banking, communications, counseling, data processing, education, engineering, environmental affairs, finance, fund raising, health services, home economics, insurance, law, library service, personnel, psychology, public relations, publishing, real estate, recreation, retailing and fashion, social work, travel agencies, urban planning.

No Experience Necessary: A Guide to Employment for the Female Liberal Arts Graduate, by Sande Friedman and Lois C. Schwartz, Dell, New York, 1971. A lively report on the employment opportunities most interesting to new college graduates which tells you some of the things you can't find out until you take the job.

Trade and Professional Associations: Career information on specific occupations is available from trade or professional associations. The most important are listed alphabetically by the italicized key word designating the field it covers.

American Institute of Certified Public *Accountants*, 666 Fifth Avenue, New York, New York 10019.

American Institute of *Aeronautics* and Astronautics, Inc., 1290 Avenue of the Americas, New York, New York 10019.

American Institute of *Architects*, 1785 Massachusetts Avenue NW, Washington, D.C. 20036.

National Association of *Bank-women*, 111 East Wacker Drive, Chicago, Illinois 60601.

American Institute of *Biological Sciences*, 3900 Wisconsin Avenue NW, Washington, D.C. 20016.

American *Chemical* Society, 1155 16th Street NW, Washington, D.C. 20036.

Society for Technical *Communications*, Inc., Suite 421, 1010 Vermont Avenue NW, Washington, D.C. 20005.

Association for *Computing* Machinery, 1133 Avenue of the Americas, New York, New York 10036.

American *Dental* Association, Council on Dental Education, 211 East Chicago Avenue, Chicago, Illinois 60611.

Division of Educational Services, American *Dental Hygienists* Association, 211 East Chicago Avenue, Chicago, Illinois 60611.

American *Dietetic* Association, 620 North Michigan Avenue, Chicago, Illinois 60611.

National *Education* Association, 1201 16th Street NW, Washington, D.C. 20036.

American Institute of Industrial *Engineers,* Inc., 345 East 47th Street, New York, New York 10017.

Society of Women *Engineers,* 345 East 47th Street, New York, New York 10017.

American Public *Health* Association, Room 901, 381 Park Avenue South, New York, New York 10016.

American *Home Economics* Association, 2010 Massachusetts Avenue NW, Washington, D.C. 20036.

American *Hospital* Association, 840 North Lake Shore Drive, Chicago, Illinois 60611.

American Institute of *Interior Designers,* 730 Fifth Avenue, New York, New York 10019.

American *Library* Association, 50 East Huron Street, Chicago, Illinois 60611.

American *Mathematical* Society, P.O. Box 6248, Providence, Rhode Island 02904.

American *Medical* Women's Association, 1740 Broadway, New York, New York 10013.

Council on *Medical Education* of the American Medical

Association, 535 North Dearborn Street, Chicago, Illinois 60610.

American Society for *Medical* Technology, Suite 200, 5555 West Loop South, Houston, Texas 77401.

Registry of *Medical* Technologists of the American Society of Clinical Pathologists, 2100 West Harrison Boulevard, Chicago, Illinois 60612.

American Guild of *Musical* Artists, 1841 Broadway, New York, New York 10023.

American *Newspaper* Publishers Association, 750 Third Avenue, New York, New York 10017.

ANA-NLN Committee on Nursing Careers, American *Nurses'* Association, 10 Columbus Circle, New York, New York 10019.

National Federation of Licensed Practical *Nurses,* Inc. 250 West 57th Street, New York, New York 10019.

American *Occupational Therapy* Association, 251 Park Avenue South, New York, New York 10010.

American *Optometric* Association, 7000 Chippewa Street, St. Louis, Missouri 63119.

American Society for *Personnel* Administration, 19 Church Street, Berea, Ohio 44017.

American *Personnel* and Guidance Association, 1607 New Hampshire Avenue NW, Washington, D.C. 20009.

American *Pharmaceutical* Association, 2215 Constitution Avenue NW, Washington, D.C. 20037.

American *Physical Therapy* Association, 1156 15th Street NW, Washington, D.C. 20005.

American Association of University *Professors,* One Dupont Circle NW, Washington, D.C. 20036.

American *Psychological* Association, 1200 17th Street NW, Washington, D.C. 20036.

The Information Center, *Public Relations* Society of America Inc., 845 Third Avenue, New York, New York 10022.

American Women in *Radio* and Television, 1321 Connecticut Avenue NW, Washington, D.C. 20036.

American Society of *Radiologic* Technologists, Suite 620, 645 North Michigan Avenue, Chicago, Illinois 60611.

National *Recreation* and Parks Association, 1601 North Kent, Arlington, Virginia 22209.

National Association of *Social Workers,* 2 Park Avenue, New York, New York 10016.

American *Speech* and Hearing Association, 9030 Old Georgetown Road, Washington, D.C. 20014.

American *Statistical* Association, 806 15th Street NW, Washington, D.C. 20005.

American Federation of *Teachers,* 1012 14th Street NW, Washington, D.C. 20005.

American *Veterinary* Medical Association, 600 South Michigan Avenue, Chicago, Illinois 60605.

Vocational Guidance: Personal advice on a career is available free to students through their high schools and colleges, and to others through state employment offices or service organizations such as the YWCA. It is also available on a fee-paid basis from both nonprofit and commercial counseling and testing agencies, or as a "free" service to members of some organizations and professional associations. The quality of counseling is erratic everywhere and depends on the chemistry of the counselor and counselee more than the sponsorship.

Many counseling organizations provide aptitude testing as a basis for their advice. These tests can suggest vocations you have not considered, but they may not be helpful to college graduates who usually come out of them slated for success in so many fields that they have as much trouble deciding what to do as before.

If your state employment office does not provide counseling or testing and can't tell you where to get it, there is a directory of women-oriented counseling programs in *Continuing Education Programs and Services for Women,* a publication of the Women's Bureau of the U.S. Department of Labor, available from the Government Printing Office, Washington, D.C. 20402, for $.70. The International Association of Counseling Services, 1607 New Hampshire Avenue NW, Washington, D.C. 20009, issues a *Directory of Approved Counseling Agencies* throughout the United States and Canada which lists types of service, hours, and fees. The directory costs $3.

Feminist Vocational Guidance: The new movement for sex equality has stimulated a new class of counseling agency specifically directed to improving the self-confidence of women who want to enter, re-enter, or upgrade themselves vocationally. Adult-education divisions of big universities have long given courses for this purpose, but feminists are organizing service agencies to do it too.

Many of the new organizations train, test, and place as well as counsel. Organizations are listed under their primary function. Examples of organizations primarily directed to counseling include:

MORE for Women Inc., Gramercy Park Hotel, 2 Lexington Avenue, New York, New York 10010. A women's career development center offering counseling for changing jobs and/or fields, establishing a vocational direction, or reentering the job market.

OPTIONS, Career Workshops for Women, Janice LaRouche, 333 Central Park West, New York, New York 10025. Career workshops and counseling sessions intended to enhance a career-minded woman's chances on the job market.

Women's Opportunities Center, Edythe R. Peters, University of California Extension, Irvine, California 92664.

Vocational Guidance for Returnees: Women going back to work after their children are grown need a special kind of vocational guidance, and a growing array of books, guides, training courses, counselors, and placement agencies undertakes to give it to them.

The best recent book for returning college graduates is *How to Go to Work When Your Husband Is Against It, Your Children Aren't Old Enough, and There's Nothing You Can Do Anyhow,* by Felice N. Schwartz, Margaret H. Schifter, and Susan S. Gillotti. Simon and Schuster, New York, 1972. Valuable for its updated and upper-middle-class, upper-middle-brow, housewife-oriented job Baedeker. Feminists complain, however, that it perpetuates the "conflict" between house and career.

The Back to Work Handbook for Housewives, by Barbara A. Prentice. Collier Books, New York, 1971, is a useful paperback guide to job opportunities for mature women who are not necessarily college graduates.

Women who want part-time work can get suggestions for the possibilities from an old, and hence hard-to-find, paperback that may be in some libraries: *380 Part-Time Jobs for Women,* by Ruth Lembeck. Dell, New York, 1968.

A voluminous literature undertakes to advise women on how to manage home and career "too." A random sampling includes:

So You Want to be a Working Mother, by Lois Benjamin. McGraw-Hill, New York, 1966, Funk and Wagnalls.

So You Want to go Back to Work, by Nanette Scofield and Betty Klarman. Random House, New York 1968.

The Working Mother, by Sidney Cornelia Callahan. Macmillan, New York, 1971; Paperback Library, 1972.

Of the many organizations serving women who want to return to work, the best-publicized is Catalyst, with national headquarters at 6 East 82nd Street, New York, New York 10028. Its primary purpose is to distribute vocational and educational self-guidance material for the family-oriented, college-oriented woman who wants to combine home duties with work. Nonprofit, and foundation funded, it has a network of resource groups that provide counseling, job referral or placement services; some are free; others charge fees.

Washington Opportunities for Women, 1111 20th Street NW, Washington, D.C. 20036, is a service for all women—black, white, college, and noncollege—affiliated with the U.S. Employment Service. It offers information and advice to women jobseekers. In 1973 WOW was helping to set up similar information centers in six other cities with the cooperation of the U.S. Employment Service.

Most cities have local organizations to aid women returning to the job market, frequently in conjunction with a nearby college or university. Typical are the Women's Opportunities Center, University of California Extension, Irvine, California 92664, and the Continuum Center, Oakland University, Rochester, Michigan 48063, which provides individual and group counseling.

EDUCATION AND TRAINING

Many women don't get paid what they're worth because their education has not been directed to the job market. Fortunately, a wide variety of educational and training facilities are now available. They include various kinds of training for specific vocations both on and off the job, and new opportunities for getting the college degree that is required for many well-paying and attractive jobs.

Continuing Education: The flowering of adult education in the 1970s is providing courses specifically designed for almost every life situation. The most comprehensive guide to what is available anywhere in the United States is: *The New York Times Guide to Continuing Education in America,* prepared by the College Entrance Examination Board, Frances Coombs

Thompson, editor, Quadrangle Books, New York, 1972. Courses are listed in two categories: classroom courses arranged alphabetically by state and then alphabetically by institutional name, and correspondence courses.

The Women's Bureau of the U.S. Department of Labor issues a directory of schools with special programs for women. Their *Continuing Education Programs and Services for Women,* Pamphlet 10, 1971, is available from the U.S. Government Printing Office, Washington, D.C. 20402 at $.70, if it is not in your local library or state employment office.

Off-Campus Degree Programs: Two organizations provide directories and information on the burgeoning programs that offer a college education to people who don't want to leave home to learn.

Special Degree Programs for Adults Exploring Non-Traditional Degree Programs in Higher Education, by Roy Troutt, dean of the College of Liberal Studies, University of Oklahoma. This booklet lists some 60 institutions with external or special degree programs, and outlines in detail the University of Oklahoma program. It may be obtained by sending $2 to American College Testing Program, Publications Division, P.O. Box 168, Iowa City, Iowa 52240.

University Without Walls: A First Report. This booklet, published in April 1972, explains how the University Without Walls program works, and notes the participating institutions. It is available at $1.75 from Dr. Samuel Baskin, president, Union for Experimenting Colleges and Universities, Antioch College, Yellow Springs, Ohio 45307.

New York State offers external degrees to anyone in the United States who can meet the requirements through courses taken at any accredited institution, and/or CLEP and CPEP examinations (see below). Write to Regents External Degrees, New York State Education Department, Room 1924, 99 Washington Avenue, Albany, New York 12210.

CLEP and CPEP stand for programs that enable mature people to get credit, by examination, for what they have learned outside of the classroom:

College Level Examination Program (CLEP), College Entrance Examination Board, 833 Seventh Avenue, New York, New York 10010. CLEP examinations are given periodically at over 300 colleges in five general and twenty-nine specific subjects for which most colleges will grant some credit.

College Proficiency Examinations (CPEP), New York State Education Department, 99 Washington Avenue, Albany, New York 12210. CPEP exams may be applied toward degrees awarded under the New York State Regents External Degree Program, which is available to everyone, not just to New York state residents.

Help is available in many cities from the local chapter of AWARE, the Association for Women's Active Return to Education, with headquarters at 5820 Wilshire Boulevard, Suite 605, Los Angeles, California 90036. The organization was formed for the purpose of encouraging women to return to school.

Women considering professions requiring advanced training beyond the bachelor's degree can get educational counseling and information on the training required for the profession of their choice through the association serving that profession, many of which are listed as sources of vocational advice beginning on page 261.

Management Training: The fastest way for a woman who already has a college degree to breach the barrier against women in top-level jobs is for her to take a few years off and get a master's degree in business administration. M.B.A.'s from Harvard, Columbia, and the Wharton School of Finance at the University of Pennsylvania go into the management job market with special prestige.

Women without the time and money for a graduate degree, who show promise on the job in a major corporation, should ask their immediate supervisors, and if necessary, the personnel department, to tell them about management training courses available at company expense. Many of these training courses include few or no women, but a query to the company's equal-employment officer should clear away any reluctance based on a woman's sex, and is likely to result in a special consideration. Companies like to report that they have women in their upper-level management programs.

An interesting development in company-paid management training is EXCEL, an American Management Association in-house course on management employees, most of whom, in offices at least, are women clerical workers. AMA Assessment Center Programs are used by employers to help identify and develop potential management talent in the ranks. Both programs have been used by government contractors to upgrade women workers as required by affirmative-action programs.

Employers who do not offer on-site management training sometimes reimburse employees who take outside courses, either at a local college or a special seminar, which have bearing on their work. Tuition reimbursement supports many short courses, workshops, and seminars ranging from one day to a week, offered under public, and both commercial and nonprofit private sponsorship.

The push for sex equality on the job has stimulated special management courses for women, offered by professional management-training organizations such as the American Management Association, as well as courses offered by women's action groups such as Federally Employed Women (FEW), an association of women in the civil service; and some of the chapters of the National Organization for Women (NOW).

A sampling of other management-training courses:

Foundation Management Seminars, sponsored by the Business and Professional Women's Foundation, 2012 Massachusetts Avenue NW, Washington, D.C. 20036. Two different seminar training courses, each limited to 125 registrants, are offered at different locations across the country throughout the year. The registration fee is $25.

Katharine Gibbs Management for Today's Woman, 200 Park Avenue, New York, New York 10017. A semester program of eight courses in management training for women who have had any combination of four years of college education, accredited business-school training, and/or business experience.

Women's Training and Resources Corporation, Congress Building, Suite 512, 142 High Street, Portland, Maine 04101. Workshops offered at different locations in the United States throughout the year. WTRC services also include placement, compliance assistance programs, and employment research.

Books on Management: The equal-opportunity movement has stimulated many books telling management how to deal with women, and women how to deal with management:

Breakthrough: Women Into Management, by Rosalind Loring and Theodora Wells. Van Nostrand Reinhold Company, New York, 1972. The most useful book of its kind.

How to Make It in a Man's World, by Letty Cottin Pogrebin. Bantam, New York, 1971. A chatty best-seller, strong on interpersonal relationships and office tactics for getting out of the female job ghetto, but the author is not above "using sex" in ways some pure feminists deplore.

The best books on the practice and language of management are, of course, those written for men on the way up, and there is nothing to prevent a woman from reading the books assigned to students in schools of business administration:

How Managers Motivate, by William Dowling and Leonard Sayles. McGraw-Hill, New York. A fine, classic primer on management.

Managing for Results, by Peter F. Drucker. Harper and Row, New York, 1964. Old but readable, and sound on the nuts-and-bolts of getting things done through others.

Less reverent accounts of how the executive suite really operates are worth a peek too:

Survival in the Executive Jungle, by Chester Burger. Macmillan, New York, 1964. An old guide to the jungle warfare and tribal customs of the bureaucracies, but eye-opening just the same.

Up the Organization, by Robert Townsend. Alfred A. Knopf, New York, 1970. Bare-knuckles advice on rising, from the president of Avis who got everyone to "try harder."

Vocational Training: One of the best ways for a woman to earn more money is to go into the male-dominated crafts, and the first step is to get the training required.

Job Training Suggestions for Women and/or Girls, Leaflet 40, Women's Bureau, available from the U.S. Government Printing Office, Washington, D.C. 20402, rounds up where to go for in-service training, apprenticeships, and government-funded manpower training.

For information on apprenticeship training, consult the nearest state employment office, or write to the United States Employment Service, U.S. Department of Labor, Washington, D.C. 20210, for the address of the apprenticeship information center nearest you.

FINDING YOUR JOB

There is an art and a craft to finding and landing a job that pays you something close to what you are worth. Much of the technique is described in the prosiest of print. The most important advice on applying for a job is not directed specifically to either sex. Good guides are available at low cost from public sources:

Merchandising Your Job Talents, U.S. Department of Labor, U.S. Government Printing Office, Washington, D.C. 20402, $.25, stock number 2900–0136. A general and valuable all-purpose handbook.

Guide to Preparing a Résumé, New York State Employment Service, U.S. Department of Labor, Albany, New York. Available at any New York State Employment office. An exceptionally good presentation of the art of résumé writing.

Many books and pamphlets are directed to women job hunters. The most useful include:

Help Wanted: Female. The Young Woman's Guide to Job-Hunting, by Alice Gore King. Charles Scribner's Sons, New York, 1968. A short, direct book distilling the author's years of experience in helping women to find jobs in New York City. Where to look, what to say, what to do.

Women at Work, by Elmer Winter. Simon and Schuster, New York 1967. Advice on job hunting and job possibilities from the president of Manpower, Inc. Older, but useful.

Job-Finding Techniques for Mature Women, Women's

Bureau, U.S. Department of Labor, pamphlet No.
11, 1970, available from the U.S. Government Printing Office, Washington, D.C. 20402 for $.30. The
basics of self-appraisal, résumé writing, interviewing, and training—good for anyone of any age

Your Job Campaign, Catalyst, 6 East 82nd Street, New
York, New York 10028. Available for $1.25. An
overview of employment possibilities for women
with families, giving detailed information on 59 careers, with entry-level requirements and job prospects. Tells you how to hunt for the job, and ends
with arguments a woman can use to convince an
employer to offer her part-time instead of full-time
work.

Suggestions for Preparing Résumés. A succinct one-page list
of do's and don'ts, with a model, available from
Women's Equity Action League, 538 National Press
Building, Washington, D.C. 20004.

Most workers actually get their jobs through friends or
friends of friends. The next most productive source is
the want-ad section of the local newspaper. If you are
interested in a special, professional field, consult the
want ads carried by its trade and professional journals.
If you know exactly what kind of job you want, try placing
a "situation wanted" ad yourself. This is particularly
good for women who want unusual hours or have exceptional, specialized skills. A "situations wanted" ad, for
instance, is the best way for a cleaning woman to get paid
the highest rate.

Placement Agencies: A recent college graduate should
get the best mileage she can out of the placement office
of her own alma mater. The specialists there can, at the

very least, advise her how to go about hunting, and supply her with leads or the names of reputable commercial employment agencies in the community where she wants to work.

Another likely source that operates free of charge is the local state employment service. Local offices vary, and the public employment services don't always get the creamiest jobs, but they do have an overall view of the local job market, and offer a wide variety of testing and counseling services that are also free or low cost.

In big cities, commercial employment agencies that charge a fee, usually part of the first paycheck, may have a near monopoly of the better jobs with big employers. They are easy to spot because they often advertise for job seekers. A woman who wants a well-paying job will do well to avoid the agencies that specialize in secretaries, because they may have nothing else.

The equal opportunity movement has stimulated the formation of employment services especially for women who want to upgrade their job status or work on a part-time basis. Many of them were started by feminists who are trying to sell the talents of women as a class to the employers they serve. Pioneering women's agencies include:

Distaffers, Incorporated, 1130 Western Savings Fund Building, Philadelphia, Pennsylvania 19107. Places professional women only, full-time or part-time, with $4 per-hour minimum salary. "The Best of Both Worlds Kit," a guide for starting a similar agency, is available for $10.

Options for Women, Inc., 8419 Germantown Avenue, Philadelphia, Pennsylvania 19118. Offers placement, counseling and testing for full-time or part-time employment; vocational guidance programs for educational institutions; community and consulting services for employers of women.

Torton Newtime Agency, 156 East 52nd Street, New York, New York 10022. Specializes in permanent positions on a 25-hour work week, and full-time management and executive-level jobs; individual assessment and informal counseling.

YOUR OWN BUSINESS

Some of the highest-paid women are in business for themselves and they all had to start sometime. To join them, a woman needs information, advice, and above all, capital. The best—and least expensive—source of information is the government.

Write to the United States Small Business Administration, 1441 L Street NW, Washington, D.C. 20416, for *Free Management Assistance Publications,* a list of some 60 pamphlets available at no cost. A companion form, SBA 115–B, lists booklets for sale.

The U.S. Department of Commerce, Washington, D.C. 20230, issues a series of *Urban Business Profiles* at $.30 each on beauty shops, bowling alleys, building-service contracting, children's and infants' wear, contract construction, contract dress manufacturing, convenience stores, custom plastics, dry cleaning, furniture stores, industrial launderers and linen supply, machine-shop job work, mobile catering, pet shops, photographic studios, real-estate brokerage, savings and loan associations, and supermarkets.

The Bank of America has a series of useful pamphlets at $1 each. Write Bank of America, *Small Business Reporter*, Department 3120, P.O. Box 37000, San Francisco, California 94137, for a free list.

A horizon-raising inventory of possibilities for women who want to run a business from their homes is provided by the case histories reported by Mary Bass Gibson in the *"Family Circle" Book of Careers at Home*, Popular Library, New York, 1971.

Up Your Own Organization: A Handbook for the Employed, Unemployed, and the Self-Employed on How to Start and Finance a New Business, by Donald M. Dible. Available from Moneysworth, 110 West 40th Street, New York, New York, 10018. An encyclopedic, nuts-and-bolts book of advice to venturers of any sex.

Advice and guidance are available, free, from the Small Business Administration, which has branches in many cities that are knowledgeable about conditions in the community. Try the phone book before writing to Washington for the branch nearest you. In addition to providing many brochures on different business subjects, SBA can lead you to business counselors, advise you where to borrow money, and, under some circumstances, make the loan themselves.

Free—but good—management advice is available through two voluntary organizations:

SCORE (Service Corps of Retired Executives), 806 Con-

necticut Avenue NW, Washington, D.C. 20525.
Offers management counseling for small businesses
through its volunteers, retired business men and
women with experience in small business administration.

ACTION-ACE (Active Corps of Executives), 806 Connecticut Avenue NW, Washington, D.C. 20525. Offers help of volunteer businessmen in planning,
coordinating, or directing a business. Ask about AC-
TION-ACE at the nearest Small Business Administration Office.

Advocates for Women, 564 Market Street, San Francisco, California 94104. A nonprofit economic development corporation funded by foundations.
Helps women who want to start a business and/or
women who are having trouble getting bank credit.

ASSERTING YOUR RIGHTS

If you are not getting equal treatment at work, you can
fight back by making a complaint or bringing a lawsuit
against the offending employer, or you can join with
others and/or support activist organizations that are
fighting for everyone similarly situated.

The first thing to do, of course, is to find out whether
your employer is really violating the law. A good general
overview of the legal situation of women in all respects
by an undoubted authority in the field:

Women and the Law, The Unfinished Revolution, by Leo

Kanowitz. Albuquerque, University of New Mexico Press, 1972.

Another good source of information by a government expert:

"Equal Pay in the United States," by Morag MacLeod Simchak. *International Labour Review,* Vol. 103, No. 6, June 1971.

The best information on specific situations are the pamphlets put out by the government agencies that enforce the laws, and they will send you the latest literature on the subject if you write asking for help. (Since they are all understaffed, that may be all they will do for some time.)

Equal Pay Facts, Leaflet 2, Women's Bureau, U.S. Department of Labor, Superintendent of Documents, Government Printing Office, Washington, D.C. 20402.

Toward Job Equality For Women, a booklet of the U.S. Equal Opportunity Commission. See also all this agency's annual reports, Government Printing Office, Washington, D.C. 20402.

The Angry Woman's Arsenal Against Sex Discrimination in Employment or How to File. A concise guide prepared by Employment Committee, New York National Organization for Women. Revised 1972.

Available through *Womanpower,* the newsletter listed on p.257. *Step by Step: Affirmative Action for Women,* $2.50.

Legal Action: If you have a complaint of sex discrimination against your employer, you can get help from Federal, state, and in some places, city, agencies, as well as from private voluntary organizations that provide different kinds of services to individuals. Below are the names and addresses of the major sources of help:

Wage and Hour Division, Employment Standards Administration, U.S. Department of Labor, 14th Street and Constitution Avenue NW, Washington, D.C. 20210. Handles complaints involving the Equal Pay Act. Complaints should be taken to the nearest office. Check telephone directory under U.S. Government, Labor Department. The complainant's name is not revealed.

U.S. Equal Employment Opportunity Commission, 1800 G Street NW, Washington, D.C. 20506. Also has regional offices in Atlanta, Chicago, Dallas, Kansas City, New York, Philadelphia, and San Francisco.

Office of Federal Contract Compliance, U.S. Department of Labor, 14th Street and Constitution Avenue NW, Washington, D.C. 20210. Also has regional offices in Boston, New York, Philadelphia, Atlanta, Chicago, Dallas, Kansas City, Denver, San Francisco, and Seattle. Area offices located in Cleveland, Detroit, Houston, New Orleans, and Los Angeles.

U.S. Civil Rights Commission, 1121 Vermont Avenue NW, Washington, D.C. 20425. Publishes reports of studies involving civil rights, including women's rights, with special emphasis on deficiencies in laws and government agencies. The commission, which has no enforcement powers, also holds hearings and refers complaints to proper agencies.

Women's Bureau, U.S. Department of Labor, 14th Street and Constitution Avenue NW, Washington, D.C. 20210. Regional offices in Boston, New York,

Philadelphia, Atlanta, Chicago, Dallas, Kansas City, Denver, San Francisco, and Seattle. The Women's Bureau publishes a variety of useful material on laws related to women's rights and sex discrimination, and on problems and opportunities for women in general. A list is available upon request. Ask for Leaflet 10, *Publications of the Women's Bureau.*

There also are various state and local agencies to which complaints may be taken. Examples of these are the New York State Division on Human Rights and the New York City Commission on Human Rights.

Legal Advice and Counseling:

Federally Employed Women, Dr. Priscilla B. Ransohoff, National Press Building, Washington, D.C. 20005. FEW provides guidance to Federally employed women in cases of sex discrimination.

Legal Defense and Education Fund, Ms. Sylvia Roberts, president, National Organization for Women, 1333 Connecticut Avenue NW, Washington, D.C. 20036. LDEF provides information on legal remedies. It also co-sponsors, with NOW, the Employment Services Discrimination Counseling Project to help women fight employment discrimination. Write to Washington Area Women's Center, 1736 R Steet NW, Washington, D.C.

Women's Equity Action League, 538 National Press Building, Washington, D.C. 20004. WEAL is a national organization which seeks to improve the status of all American women through education, legislation, and litigation. It has sued universities and government agencies. WEAL's *Washington Re-*

port is one of the best sources of information on new legislation affecting women.

Human Rights for Women, 1128 National Press Building, Washington, D.C. 20004. Provides free legal assistance in landmark cases to women meeting sex discrimination, undertakes research and studies concerning women's roles and their present social and economic conditions.

Women's Law Fund, 620 Keith Building, 1621 Euclid Avenue, Cleveland, Ohio 44115. Funds litigation involving sex discrimination in employment, but its staff is limited to two full-time attorneys with part-time and volunteer help.

Affiliates of the American Civil Liberties Union located in each state, with the aid of ACLU's Women's Rights Project, offer legal advice on issues that affect constitutional rights, and are helpful on extra-legal remedies as well.

Midwest Women's Legal Group, 54 West Randolph Street, Room 902, Chicago, Illinois 60601. Provides legal help for women with special emphasis on welfare recipients, indigents, lesbians, working-class women. Lay-advocacy programs, self-help information, and in some cases, legal advice and counseling by attorneys.

Collective Action: Whatever your complaint, the chances are that it is not unique. Scores or perhaps hundreds of other women are likely to be concerned about the same thing. Sometimes the best way to upgrade a category or accelerate promotion opportunities is to join or form an organization of fellow workers actively seeking the same goal.

Called caucuses, alliances, committees, or councils, hundreds of such groups have been formed. Some are composed of women who work for the same company. For others the bond may be a common occupation, industry, or geographical area.

Professional women, especially those in academic disciplines, are exceptionally well-organized. Caucuses exist for women architects, economists, planners, guidance counselors, construction workers, archivists, among many others. For a full listing from which a woman student or professional can choose, write Bernice Sandler, director, Project on the Status and Education of Women, Association of American Colleges, 1818 R. Street NW, Washington, D.C. 20009

Especially active groups working for special occupations include:

National Committee on Household Employment, Ms. Edith Sloan, 1625 Eye Street NW, Washington, D.C. 20006. A foundation-funded group serving the most oppressed workers—domestics. Working women who employ household help should consult its code of standards. An organization that deserves the support of every woman.

Federal Women's Program, 300 South Wacker Drive, attention Annette Adams, D.O.L., Chicago, Illinois 60606. Composed of Federal women workers and dedicated to abolishing sexism in the Federal service. Mails a package of organizing materials for $1.

National Conference on Black Women, Box 193, Pittsburgh, Pennsylvania 15230. Works to improve economic opportunities for black women. Matches jobs and people and presses for affirmative action programs.

Union Women's Alliance to Gain Equality, president, Anne Lipow, 2137 Oregon Street, Berkeley, California 94707. Women trade unionists dedicated to equal rights, pay, and opportunities, also paid maternity leaves with no loss of seniority and adequate medical coverage, and child-care facilities— "employer and government supported; parent-staff controlled."

American Federation of Teachers, Women's Rights Committee, 1012 14th Street NW, Washington, D.C.

Midwest Women's Legal Group, 54 West Randolph, Room 902, Chicago, Illinois 60601.

National Education Association, Women's Caucus, 1201 16th Street NW, Washington, D.C. 20036. Aims to improve status of women "within the education profession."

Chicago Women in Publishing, P.O. Box 392, Morton Grove, Illinois 60053. Formed "to improve the status of women in publishing and related fields."

Women Involved, 1572 Massachusetts Avenue, Cambridge, Massachusetts 02138. Works with "groups of women in public and private institutions to improve their status and help their institutions better address the needs of women."

Federally Employed Women, 621 National Press Building, Washington, D.C. 20004. Monitors progress of women in Federal Civil Service and aims to accelerate it.

SERVICES TO MANAGEMENT

The business press and specialized advisories to management issued by such organizations as the American Management Association have been paying a great deal of editorial attention to the problem of complying with the new tough sex equality laws and regulations. The laws were so general in terms, and changing so fast, that they were creating a market for specialized books, newsletters, guides, conferences, seminars, counseling services, training courses, "talent banks"—rosters of qualified women to fill high-level posts, and executive search enterprises.

Many of those in the best position to supply these management services were feminists who quite properly expected to be paid for helping employers comply with the spirit and letter of the sex equality laws.

Some of the services recently available to management include:

The Association of Feminist Consultants, with about fifty members all over the country, was a good source of consultants. Dr. Jennifer S. Macleod, 4 Canoe Brook Drive, Princeton Junction, New Jersey 08550, has been coordinator for the Association.

Boyle Kirkman Associates, Inc., 230 Park Avenue, New York, New York 10028, was founded by Barbara Boyle, IBM's pioneer equal-employment-opportunity specialist for women. This firm assists companies in utilizing women resources more effectively. Areas of assistance include personnel procedures, executive EEO presentations, training programs for women, management awareness seminars, and career counseling management workshops. Boyle Kirkman's video-tape, "Women: The Emerging Resource," is available from Advance Systems, Inc., 15 Columbus Circle, New York, New York 10019.

Betsy Hogan Associates, 222 Rawson Road, Brookline, Massachusetts 02146, are "management consultants on the compliance, cultural, legal, and organizational problems of women in employment." Surveys of company practices, conferences and seminars for middle managers, first-line supervisors, and promotable women. Publishes *Womanpower*.

Danforth-Clare Company, Inc., 10 Columbus Circle, New York, New York 10019, Patricia Haskell, executive vice-president. Publishes an affirmative action compliance guide for employers.

Urban Research Corporation, 5464 South Shore Drive, Chicago, Illinois 60615. Susan Davis, a vice-president of Urban Research Corporation and publisher of *The Spokeswoman*, headed a team of four feminists who gave conferences for corporate personnel executives on equal employment practices.

Women's Training and Resources Corporation, Congress Building, 142 High Street, Suite 512, Portland, Maine 04101, headed by Ko Kimmel, offers programs in the areas of compliance-assistance and training for professional women, such as "Breaking Barriers through Speech."

Womanpower Consultants, 2223 B Roosevelt Avenue, Berkeley, California 94703. Consulting on affirmative-action programming, policy development, and training. Works with both employer and employee groups.

Wells Christie Associates, Theodora Wells, Lee Christie, P.O. Box 3392, Beverly Hills, California 90212. Consultants for changes in organizational and male-female relationships as equal opportunity changes women's work roles.

Executive Search: Employers are actively searching for qualified women for high-level positions in part at least to show compliance authorities that they are taking the "affirmative action" required by law. Traditional executive-search firms are handicapped because they have systematically ignored qualified women candidates in the past, so corporate managers are turning to new search organizations headed by qualified women who know where to find other qualified women.

All the feminist consultants and employment agencies already listed will undertake talent searches at a fee if they do not have the talent required in their files. A few of the organizations specializing in the recruitment of professional and executive women include:

Fordyce Andrews & Haskell, Inc., 230 Park Avenue, New York, New York 10017. An established executive-search firm with a special division headed by Elizabeth Weld recruits women executives in manufacturing, engineering, industrial relations, and data processing. Mrs. Weld welcomes résumés of qualified women.

McKay and Associates, 406 Westwood Drive, Chapel Hill, North Carolina 27514. Martha McKay was the consultant who located a woman for the AT&T board of directors.

RLS Associates, 41 Broad Street, Charleston, South Carolina 29407. Ms. Barbara DeMarco. Sponsors "Career Weekends" for women, bringing women qualified for jobs in management, personnel, sales, marketing, research, computer applications, accounting, and engineering together with company recruiters.

Rosters and "Talent Banks": The stock complaint of male chauvinists has been that they "can't find" women qualified for high-level posts. This is true in part because women have not been visible, and no comprehensive lists of competent women exist. In order to help employers comply with equal opportunity laws and implement affirmative action programs, women's organizations in politics, business, and the professions have been busy compiling "talent banks" for the use of employers. Rosters have been compiled in almost every field of endeavor. The most publicized was compiled for the use of President Nixon in making Federal appointments by Barbara Franklin, his staff assistant for the recruitment of women.

A sampling of organizations with talent banks or job-referral facilities:

Alliance of Women in Architecture, 18 East 13 Street, New York, New York 10003.

American Society of Planning Officials, 1313 East 60th Street, Chicago, Illinois 60637.

American Association of Immunologists, Dr. Helen C.

Rauch, Department of Medical Microbiology, Stanford University School of Medicine, Stanford, California 94305.

American Political Science Association, Committee on the Status of Women in the Profession, 1527 New Hampshire Avenue NW, Washington, D.C. 20036.

Association of Women in Science, Dr. Susan G. Longreth, Rockefeller University, New York, New York 10021.

Biophysical Society and Association of Women in Science, 5,000 women engineers, scientists, medical and paramedical specialists. Dr. Marion Webster, 2226 Broadbranch Terrace, Washington, D.C. 20008.

Black Women's Association of Pittsburgh, P.O. Box 193, Pittsburgh, Pennsylvania 15230. Elizabeth M. Scott, president.

Boston Theological Institute, Women's Placement Service, Elizabeth Dempster, 45 Francis Avenue, Cambridge, Massachusetts 02138. Women qualified to teach religion and related fields.

The Cooperative College Registry, One DuPont Circle NW, Suite 10, Washington, D.C. 20036. Faculty and administrative positions in higher education.

Federally Employed Women. Dr. Priscilla B. Ransohoff, National Press Building, Washington, D.C. 20005

Feminist Studio Workshop, 2901 Waverly Drive, Los Angeles, California 90039. Registry and slides of women artists and designers.

Individual Resources, 60 East 12 Street, New York, New York 10003. Non-profit, free computer-based employment and counseling service for all kinds of talent.

Interstate Association of Commissions on the Status of Women, Joy R. Simonson, District Building, 14th and E Street NW, Washington, D.C. 20004, for information on rosters compiled by member commissions in the various states.

McKay and Associates, 406 Westwood Drive, Chapel Hill, North Carolina 27514.

The National Federation of Business and Professional Women's Clubs, Inc, 2012 Massachusetts Avenue NW, Washington, D.C. 20036.

National Organization for Women Employment Task Force, Wilma Scott Heide, President, 1957 East 73rd Street, Chicago, Illinois 60649.

Women's Equity Action League (WEAL), 538 National Press Building, Washington, D.C. 20004. Rosters are being compiled by some state chapters.

Women's Caucus—Religious Studies, Box 6309, Station B, Vanderbilt University, Nashville, Tennessee 37235. Two hundred names of women in academic religious studies.

Index

typing, need for, 87–8
typist jobs, 67, 70

Uccello, Antonina P., 65
unemployment: insurance, maternity, 219; men, 137–8; women, 55, 251–2
uniforms, 146
unions, 227–39; antiunionism, 244; apprenticeships, 179–85; benefits, 228; craft businesses and, 157–9; discrimination, 187–8, 235; disputes and negotiations, 14; feminist activism, 233–8; grievance machinery, 232–4; leadership, 235–8; membership, women, 178–9, 228; organizing, 238–9; seniority, 216–17; wages and salaries, 178, 216–17, 227, 232–3; women's rights, 230–4
United Air Lines, 123
United Auto Workers, 230–2
United Parcel Service, 224
University of California, Berkeley, 248–9
Upward Mobility, 54
Urban League, 181

veterans preference, 52
vocational guidance: aptitude tests, 40–1, 63, 82–3, 180–2; counseling, 41–2, 59; informa-

tion sources, 259–68, 274; return to work, 63–4, 266–8
volunteer work, 64–6

Wage and Hour Division, 104, 201
wages. *See* salaries and wages
waitresses, 56–7
Walsh, Julia, 62
Washington Post, 107, 245
weather research, 24, 35
Weed, Lois, 91
Weiner, Ruth, 133
Weisenborn, Clara, 249–50
Weiss, Bonnie, 148
Weld, Elizabeth, 129
welding, 17
welfare, internal corporate, 37–8
welfare, public, 36–7, 43–4; vocational training programs, 186–7
Wertheimer, Barbara, 231, 233
Westwood, Jean, 26
Weyand, Ruth, 233
Wheaton Glass Co., 203–4
Wheeler, Bonnie and Robert, 133
Whyte, William H., 83
Willoughby, Darlene, 29
Women's Caucus of the National Lawyers Guild, 249
Women's Liberation Movement, 18–19, 26–7, 231, 243
Workers Defense League, 181